The latest Ninja

Foodi Possible Cooker

Cookbook 2024

2000 Days of No-Stress and Delicious Ninja Foodi PossibleCooker Recipes for Beginners to Make Your Meals Taste Fabulous

Julieta R. Reeves

Contents

Chapter VIII Appetizer Recipes 61

Chapter IX Sweet snacks and desserts Recipes 69

INTRODUCTION

• What is the Ninja Foodi Possible Cooker PRO?

The Ninja Foodie Cooker PRO is that kitchen appliance that comes to your rescue whenever needed. It is like the superhero you never knew you needed in your kitchen. This 8 in 1 multi-cooker can replace 14 cooking utensils—from cooker to oven to steamer—you name it! It's literally like your kitchen's Swiss army knife!

• Why choose the Ninja Foodi Possible Cooker PRO?

Aside from being a powerhouse multi-cooker, it comes in a sea-salt gray color, which matches any color you have in your kitchen. Also, it has a capacity of 8.5 Quarts, so you have ample space to cook your comfort food in this all-in-one cooker.

• The Benefits of the Ninja Foodi Possible Cooker PRO

The benefits are endless with this nonstick pot, however, here are some key ones:

1. It is versatile with its 8-in-1 multifunction
2. It is nonstick and oven-safe
3. It has an integrated glass lid and comes with a spoon
4. It weighs just 13lb (even with all its functions)
5. It can handle a temperature of up to 500°F
6. Finally, it comes with an inspiring cookbook.

• How to Clean the Ninja Foodi Possible Cooker PRO

1. Cleaning up after cooking doesn't have to be tiresome. The Ninja Foodi Possible Cooker PRO is quite easy to clean. Here's how to do it without breaking a sweat:
2. Let it cool down after use
3. After it cools, you can handwash it or throw it in the dishwasher, whichever rocks your boat! It's nonstick, so there's no need to scrub.
4. That was fast. Now you can get back to enjoying your meals.

• Possible Risks

Though every superhero has its weak parts, the Ninja Foodi Possible Cooker PRO has those too, but is safe. Here:

● Its weight of 13 lbs. could be a lot for you if move it around often

● It could get hot, so be mindful of its hot surface (use oven mitts)

• Tips and Tricks to Using the Ninja Foodi Possible Cooker PRO

1. You can pull off kitchen magic like a pro with a few tricks in your bag. Here are some tips:
2. Make the most of multi-cooking by combining ingredients in one-pot meals
3. Layer your ingredients for layered flavor
4. Get consistent and quick results by preheating
5. Don't open it constantly while cooking. Use the glass lid to monitor instead.
6. Cook meals faster and make them more flavorful by playing with the pressure
7. Last but not least, play with cooking times as well. You can choose yours. It's yours!

• FAQs

Can I use th e Ninja Foodi Possible Cooker PRO for baking?

Absolutely! Its oven-safe pot is multifunctional

Can I use metal utensils with the nonstick pot?

It's best to use non-metal utensils to keep the pot in shape.

Can I steam vegetables in the Ninja Foodi Possible Cooker PRO?

Absolutely! Its steaming function works like magic and preserves your nutrients, keeping your veggies healthy.

Does it come with a cookbook?

Yes, it does! The Ninja Foodi Possible Cooker PRO comes with an inspiring cookbook to get you started on your cooking.

Is there a warranty for the Ninja Foodi Possible Cooker PRO?

Yes, the Ninja Foodi Possible Cooker PRO comes with a warranty. Check the details in the manual for the terms and warranty period.

Chapter I Breakfast Recipes

SCRAMBLED EGGS WITH TOAST

Serves 2 / Prep time: 7 minutes / Cook time: 8 minutes

- 4 slices bread (preferably white, sourdough bread)
- 4 eggs
- Chopped parsley or dill to garnish
- 1 tbsp butter
- 0.67 cup good quality feta cheese crumbles

1. Spread a thin layer of softened butter on both sides of the bread.
2. Fry the bread over medium heat for about 2 minutes on each side until a golden brown crust forms. Alternatively, you can use the Ninja Foodi PossibleCooker Oven toaster to toast your bread.
3. Remove the bread from the frying pan and add ½ tbsp. of butter.
4. Add the eggs and feta cheese and cook on medium-low heat, stirring often, for about 3-4 minutes, until the eggs are cooked. (Add salt to taste)
5. Divide the eggs between the bread slices and sprinkle them with freshly chopped dill or parsley.

Per Serving: Calories: 462 / Fat: 27g / Carbs: 29g / Fiber: 2g / Protein: 24g

FRESH FRUIT AND GREEK YOGURT PARFAIT WITH GRANOLA

Serves 2 / Prep time: 5 minutes

- 1½ cups plain Greek yogurt (approx. 12 ounces)
- 1 cup granola (any flavor such as oats and honey or oats and chocolate)
- 1½ cups fresh berries (washed and dried, or any fresh fruit of choice)
- 1 teaspoon vanilla extract
- 1-2 tablespoons honey

1. In a small bowl, combine the Greek yogurt and vanilla extract. Mix these contents thoroughly until well combined.
3. Layer the Greek yogurt and berries in another bowl or glass jar, ¾ cup each per serving.
4. Top with ½ cup granola per serving and drizzle with honey.
5. Serve or cover tightly and store in the refrigerator for up to 3 days for best results.

Per Serving: Calories: 511 / Fat: 15g / Carbs: 71g / Fiber: 6g / Protein: 25g

PORRIDGE WITH HONEY AND BERRIES

Serves 4 / Prep time: 10 minutes/ Cook time: 25 minutes

- 600 ml Milk
- 200 g oats
- 100 g blueberries
- 2 tbsp. vanilla sugar
- 4 strawberries
- 2 tbsp. honey (or to taste,

1. Combine milk, vanilla sugar, and oats and boil while stirring.
2. Simmer, stirring occasionally, for 10-15 minutes on low heat, until creamy.
3. Add milk, if necessary, and pour into bowls.
4. Rinse the berries and pat them dry.
5. Halve strawberries if needed.
6. Top porridge with berries and drizzle with honey to taste.

Per Serving: Calories: 350 / Fat: 9g / Carbs: 54g / Fiber: 6.3g / Protein: 12g

MAPLE PANCAKES

Serves 6 / Prep time: 20 minutes / Cook time: 10 minutes

- 3 cups all-purpose flour
- 1-1 / 2 teaspoons salt
- 2-1 / 4 cups 2% milk
- 3 tablespoons maple syrup
- Optional: Additional maple syrup, butter and fresh blueberries
- 4-1 / 2 teaspoons baking powder
- 3 large eggs, room temperature
- 1 / 3 cup canola oil

1. In a large bowl, combine flour, baking powder, and salt.
2. Whisk eggs, milk, oil, and syrup in another bowl; stir into the dry ingredients until blended.
3. Preheat the griddle over medium heat. Lightly grease the griddle.
4. Pour batter by 1 / 4 cupful onto the griddle; cook until bubbles on top begin to pop and bottoms are golden brown.
5. Turn; cook until the second side is golden brown (pancakes will be thin).
6. Serve with additional maple syrup, butter, and blueberries, as desired.

Per Serving: Calories: 445 / Fat: 17g / Carbs: 59g / Fiber: 2g / Protein: 13g

AVOCADO TOAST WITH POACHED EGG

Serves 2 / Prep time: 2 minutes / Cook time: 8 minutes

- 4 eggs
- 2 / 3 avocado
- Salt and pepper for topping
- 4 slices whole grain bread
- 4 tablespoons shaved Parmesan cheese

1. Boil water in a pot to a boil. Drop the metal rims (outer rim only) of two mason jar lids into the pot so they lie flat on the bottom.
3. Turn off the heat and carefully crack the eggs directly into each rim when the water is boiling.
4. Cover the pot and poach for 5 minutes. While the eggs cook, toast the bread and smash the avocado on each piece of toast.
6. When the eggs are done, use a spatula to lift the eggs out of the water. Gently pull the rim off of the eggs and place the poached eggs on top of the toast.
7. Sprinkle with Parmesan cheese, salt, pepper, and fresh herbs; serve with the fresh quartered heirloom tomatoes.

Per Serving: Calories: 393 / Fat: 20.4g / Carbs: 30.1g / Fiber: 7.7g / Protein: 23.3g

BANANA NUT MUFFINS

Serves 15 / Prep time: 15 minutes / Cook Time: 15 minutes

- ½ cup unsalted butter
- 2 large eggs
- 2 teaspoons pure vanilla extract
- 1 teaspoon baking soda
- ½ cup of chopped walnuts
- ⅔ cup brown sugar
- 2 cups mashed bananas
- 1 ¾ cup of all-purpose flour
- ¼ teaspoon

1. Heat the oven to 350°F. In a large bowl, whisk melted butter and ⅔ cup brown sugar until it's well combined. Add eggs, mashed banana, and vanilla, then whisk.
2. Mix flour, baking soda, salt, and cinnamon in another bowl.
3. Add dry ingredients to the wet ingredients, and stir it with a rubber spatula. Add ½ cup chopped nuts and stir until no streaks of flour remain.
4. Grease 15 standard-sized muffin cups and divide the batter evenly among the cups.
5. Sprinkle the top of each cup with brown sugar and chopped walnuts (topping).
6. Bake for 14-17 minutes, Place the pan on a wire rack to cool.

Per Serving: Calories: 231 / Fat: 10g / Carbs: 32g / Fiber: 2g / Protein: 3g /

BREAKFAST BURRITO WITH EGGS, SAUSAGE, AND CHEESE

Serves 4 / Prep time: 20 mins/ Cook time: 30 mins

- 4 ounces hot pork sausage
- 5 eggs
- salt and pepper
- 1/2 cup salsa
- 1/2 cup cheddar cheese (shredded)
- 3 large flour tortillas

1. Cook sausage in a medium-hot skillet until no longer pink, add salsa, and cook until most of the liquid is gone.
2. In another skillet, scramble eggs lightly. Before they are completely done, add to the sausage / salsa mixture and set aside.
3. Heat flour tortillas in a large skillet over high heat, turning twice and heating until the tortilla is soft.

4. Place the warm, flexible tortilla on the serving plate, add 1 / 4 portion of egg / sausage mix to the tortilla, top with 1 / 8 cup cheddar cheese, and then roll burro style.

5. If you like more spice, serve with more salsa, sour cream, and cilantro.

Per Serving: Calories: 987 / Carbs: 23g / Protein:53g / Fat: 75 g / Fiber: 2g

SMOOTHIE BOWL WITH SPINACH, BANANA, AND ALMOND MILK

Serves 2 / Prep time: 5mins

- 1 / 4 cup almond milk
- 1 / 2 small avocado
- 1 cup frozen mango
- 1 tablespoon almond butter
- 1 cup packed spinach
- 1 frozen banana
- 1 tablespoon ground flax

1. Place almond milk, spinach, avocado, banana, and mango into the blender
2. Blend until smooth. Smoothies should be thick, not watery
3. Pour the smoothies into two small bowls and top each with ground flax and almond butter.
4. Serve with a spoon and enjoy immediately.

Per Serving: Calories: 238 / Carbs: 31g / Protein: 4g / Fat: 12g / Fiber: 7g

BAGEL WITH CREAM CHEESE AND SMOKED SALMON

Serves 2 / Prep time: 10mins

- 2 bagels halved
- 4 ounces cream cheese
- 1 tablespoon fresh dill plus more for serving
- 1-2 Persian cucumbers peeled in ribbons
- Capers to taste
- 4 ounces smoked salmon thinly sliced
- 2 tablespoons lemon juice
- Salt and pepper to taste
- Red onion slices for serving

1. In a small bowl, combine the cream cheese, lemon juice, fresh dill, and salt and pepper to taste.
2. Toast the bagels. Spread the cream cheese mixture on both sides of the bagel.
3. Add the cucumbers, smoked salmon, capers, and red onion to the bottom of the toasted bagels.
4. Top with the top of the bagels and enjoy

Per Serving: Calories: 577 / Carbs: 64g / Protein: 26g / Fat: 24g / Fiber: 4g

VEGGIE OMELETTE WITH TOMATOES, PEPPERS, AND CHEESE

Serves 1 / Prep time: 10 mins/ Cook time: 10mins

- 1 / 3 cup chopped green pepper
- 2 teaspoons olive oil
- 3 eggs
- 1 / 8 teaspoon salt
- 1 / 3 cup chopped tomato
- 2 tablespoons chopped onion
- 1 tablespoon butter
- 3 tablespoons water
- 1 / 8 teaspoon pepper

1. In a small nonstick skillet, sauté green pepper and onion in oil until tender. Remove from the skillet and set aside.
2. In the same skillet, melt butter over medium-high heat.
3. Whisk the eggs, water, salt, and pepper, then add the egg mixture to the skillet (mixture should set immediately at the edges).
4. As eggs are set, push cooked edges toward the center, letting uncooked portions flow underneath.
5. When the eggs are set, spoon the green pepper mixture and tomato on one side; fold the other side over the filling.
6. Slide the omelet onto a plate.

Per Serving: Calories: 424 / Carbs: 8g / Protein: 20g / Fat: 35g / Fiber: 2g

FRENCH TOAST WITH POWDERED SUGAR

Serves 8 / Prep time: 5mins/ Cook time: 10mins

- 4 large eggs
- 1 / 4 cup all-purpose flour
- 2 / 3 cup milk
- 1 / 4 cup granulated sugar

- 1 / 4 teaspoon salt
- 1 teaspoon vanilla extract
- 1 teaspoon ground cinnamon
- 8 thick slices of bread

1. Preheat the griddle to 350 degrees or heat a skillet over medium heat.
2. Add all ingredients, except the bread, to a blender or a shallow dish and whisk well to combine.
3. If whisking is by hand, mix flour and eggs first, then add the remaining ingredients.
4. Dip bread slices into the batter, dredging them well on both sides, and place on a hot, greased griddle or skillet.
5. Cook for a few minutes, until the bottom of the bread starts to get golden brown. Flip and cook on the other side the same way.
6. Remove to a plate. Serve warm with syrup and a sprinkle of powdered sugar.

Per Serving: Calories: 89 / Carbs: 11g / Protein: 4g / Fat: 3g / Fiber: 0.3g

PEANUT BUTTER AND BANANA SANDWICH

Serves 1 / Prep time: 5mins/ Cook time: 5mins
- 2 tablespoons peanut butter
- 1 medium banana, sliced
- 2 slices whole wheat bread
- cooking spray

1. Spread 1 tablespoon of peanut butter on one piece of bread. Arrange the banana slices on the same piece of bread.
2. Spread the remaining peanut butter on the second piece of bread.
3. Invert the second piece of bread and place it over the bananas so that you have the banana between the two slices, and press firmly.
4. Heat skillet slightly. Spray a skillet with cooking spray and heat over medium heat.
5. Place the sandwich on the hot skillet and cook until golden brown, 2 to 3 minutes per side.
6. Serve in a plate and enjoy with any drink of your choice

Per Serving: Calories: 437 / Carbs: 57g / Protein: 17g / Fat: 19g / Fiber: 9g

CHIA SEED PUDDING WITH COCONUT MILK AND BERRIES

Serves 4 / Prep time: 7 mins / Inactive time: 2hrs
- 1 cup of unsweetened coconut milk (the lower-fat refrigerated kind, such as Silk – not canned)
- 1 / 4 cup chia seeds
- 1 tablespoon sugar
- 1 tablespoon of pure maple syrup
- 1 / 2 teaspoon vanilla
- 1 / 4 cup blackberry jelly or preServes (preferably 100% pure fruit, such as Smucker's Simply Fruit)
- 1 cup of fruit (blueberries, sliced strawberries, and sliced bananas; see note)
- 1 / 4 cup of granola (such as Cascadian Farm Oats & Honey)

1. Mix coconut milk, chia seeds, maple syrup, sugar, and vanilla in a medium bowl. Whisk to combine.
2. Set aside for 10 mins then whisk again to break up clumps of chia seeds
3. Cover with plastic wrap and refrigerate for at least an hour. You can divide it into 4 single-serve containers.

Per Serving: Calories: 179 / Carbs: 32g / Protein: 3g / Fat: 5g / Fiber: 6g

BREAKFAST QUESADILLA WITH HAM AND CHEESE

Serves 6 / Prep time: 10 mins/ Cook time: 30 mins
- 8 large eggs
- ½ teaspoon salt
- 3 tablespoons butter, softened, divided
- 2 cups shredded Cheddar cheese
- 1 tablespoon water
- ½ teaspoon pepper
- 6 (8 inch) whole wheat tortillas
- 1 (8-ounce) package of Ham

1. Whisk eggs, water, salt, and pepper in a medium bowl until well blended. Melt 1 tablespoon butter in a medium nonstick skillet over medium heat.
2. Cook eggs, stirring frequently, until scrambled to the desired consistency. Transfer to a bowl and set aside.
3. Spread 1 teaspoon butter over 1 tortilla and place butter-side down in the same skillet over medium heat.
4. Sprinkle 1 / 3 cup cheese over the entire tortilla; add 1 / 2 cup scrambled egg and 1 / 3 cup ham to one-

half.
5. Cook for 3 minutes until the cheese is melted then, fold the cheese side over the egg-ham filling, then flip the quesadilla.
6. Cook for 2 more minutes until golden and toasted.
Per Serving: Calories: 418 / Carbs: 29g / Protein: 28g / Fat: 25g / Fiber: 3g

BLUEBERRY WAFFLES WITH WHIPPED CREAM

Serves 6 / Prep time: 10 mins/ Cook time: 20 mins

- 3 eggs
- ¾ cup butter
- 3 teaspoons baking powder
- 1 ½ tablespoon sugar
- 1 teaspoon almond extract
- 1 cup heavy whipping cream
- ½ teaspoon vanilla extract
- 2 ¼ cups milk
- 3 cups sifted flour
- ¾ teaspoons salt
- 1 ½ cup fresh blueberries
- ½ teaspoon vanilla extract
- ¼ cup powdered sugar

1. Put the egg whites and yolks in separate bowls. Beat the egg whites till they are stiff.
2. Beat the egg yolks, add melted butter and milk then mix. Mix the two extracts until well combined.
3. Mix sifted flour, baking powder, ingredients, and egg yolk in another bowl and whisk until smooth.
4. Fold in blueberries and egg whites until well combined, Bake in a hot waffle iron until slightly brown and crispy.
5. Beat the whipping cream quickly, slowly adding the powdered sugar. Add the extract and beat until it forms soft peaks
Per Serving: Calories: 616 / Carbs: 93g / Protein: 13g / Fat: 22g / Fiber: 2g

COTTAGE CHEESE AND PINEAPPLE BOWL

Serves 2 / Prep time:10 mins

- 250 grams of cottage cheese
- 1 tablespoon honey
- 1 pineapple

1. Crumble the cottage cheese roughly, place it in a bowl, and set aside.
2. Chop the pineapple into the desired shape and size and add it to the bowl with crumbled cottage cheese.
3. Mix honey to the cottage cheese bowl until well combined. Make sure you coat the pineapple as well as cottage cheese with honey.
4. Serve it immediately with a glass of fresh juice and enjoy!
Per Serving: Calories: 244 / carbs: 18g / Protein: 17g / Fats: 12g / Fiber: 3g

BREAKFAST WRAP WITH SCRAMBLED EGGS, BLACK BEANS, AND SALSA

Serves 12 / Prep time: 25 mins/ Cook time: 35 mins

- 2 tablespoon avocado oil
- Non-stick vegetable spray
- 1 / 4 teaspoon Kosher salt
- 1 / 4 cup unsweetened almond milk
- 1 red pepper, diced
- 1 can black beans, rinsed
- 8 ounces cheddar cheese
- 3 cups shredded hash brown potatoes
- 7 large eggs, lightly beaten
- Ground black pepper
- 12 ounces plant-based beef
- 16 ounces of chunky salsa
- 12 large tortilla wraps

1. Heat the avocado oil in a skillet, add the Hash Brown Potatoes, and cook until golden brown.
2. Whisk the eggs, salt, pepper, and almond milk, and spray the skillet with non-stick spray. Pour in the egg mixture and scramble the eggs. Set aside.
3. Heat the avocado oil, add the beef, and sauté over medium heat until browned. Add the diced red pepper and sauté until softened.
4. Pour in the chunky salsa, stir till the liquid reduces, and remove the pan from the fire. Brush the edges of a tortilla with beaten eggs
5. Put Salsa Beef, browned Hash Browns, scrambled egg, black beans, and cheddar cheese at the bottom of

the totilla. Roll the tortilla up and press down the end to adhere.
6. Heat a thin layer of avocado oil in a clean skillet. Place burritos in the oil and fry until they're browned on each side.

Per Serving: Calories: 234 / Carbs: 17g / Protein: 14g / Fat: 13g / Fiber: 6g

SPINACH AND FETA QUICHE

Serves 8 / Prep time: 15 mins/ Cook time: 55 mins

- 2 tablespoons extra-virgin olive oil
- 2 cloves garlic, minced
- 1 ¼ cups reduced-fat milk
- 1 tablespoon chopped fresh dill
- 1 teaspoon salt
- 3 ounces crumbled feta cheese
- ½ cup finely chopped onion
- 1 package chopped spinach, thawed and squeezed dry
- 4 large eggs, beaten
- 1 teaspoon lemon zest
- ¼ teaspoon ground pepper

1. Preheat the oven to 325°F. Lightly coat a 9-inch pie pan with cooking spray.
2. Heat oil in a large skillet over medium heat. Add onion and cook, stirring, until softened, about 3 minutes.
3. Add garlic and cook, stirring, until fragrant. Stir in spinach; remove from heat. Whisk milk, eggs, dill, lemon zest, salt, and pepper in a bowl.
4. Spread the mixture evenly in the pie pan, sprinkle with feta, then add the egg mixture.
5. Bake until a knife inserted comes out dry, 45 minutes.

Per Serving: Calories: 126 / Carbs: 5g / Protein: 7g / Fat: 9g / Fiber: 1g

ENGLISH MUFFIN WITH BACON AND EGG

Serves 2 / Prep time: 5mins/ Cook time: 15 mins

- Large Frying Pan
- Large Plate
- 4 slices of Bacon
- 2 square slices of American processed Cheese
- Hot Sauce
- Plastic Spatula
- 2 English Muffins, halved
- 4 Eggs
- 1 tbsp Butter
- Salt and black Pepper

1. Add bacon to a pan over medium heat and fry until crispy. Remove bacon, and leave fat.
2. Increase heat. Lace English muffin halves in the leftover fat and fry until crispy. Remove from the pan.
3. Lower heat and melt in 1 tbsp butter. Spread it across the pan, then crack in 4 eggs.
4. Use your spatula to separate the eggs into pairs then season with salt and pepper. Cook until all egg white turns opaque
5. Place muffin halves over the eggs, flip the muffin over from the pan to a plate
6. Add a slice of cheese, 2 slices of bacon and hot sauce to each. Fold over and enjoy!

Per Serving: Calories: 573 / Carbs: 29.12g / Protein: 26.47g / Fat: 39.19g / Fiber: 2.8g

SAUSAGE AND HASH BROWNS CASSEROLE

Serves 8 / Prep time: 20 mins/ Cook time: 1hr,10mins

- 20 ounces shredded hash browns thawed
- ¼ cup onion finely diced
- ½ green bell pepper diced
- 8 eggs
- ½ teaspoon Kosher salt
- 1 pound sausage cooked, crumbled, and drained
- ½ red bell pepper diced
- 2 cups cheddar cheese shredded
- 1 can evaporated milk
- ¼ teaspoon black pepper

1. Preheat the oven to 350°F. Grease a 9×13 inch pan. Heat a large skillet over medium-high heat.
2. Brown the sausage until no pink remains. Drain fat.
3. In the prepared pan, add the hashbrowns, cooked sausage, onions, bell peppers, and 1 ½ cups of cheese, mix and spread evenly in the pan.
4. Add the eggs, evaporated milk, salt & pepper in a large bowl, then whisk until well combined.
5. Pour the egg mixture over the hash brown mixture and sprinkle the remaining cheese.
6. Cover the dish with foil and bake for 55-65 minutes until cooked.

Per Serving: Calories: 474 / Carbs: 19g / Protein: 25g / Fat: 33 g / Fiber: 1g

APPLE CINNAMON PANCAKES

Serves 4 / Prep time: 10 mins/ Cook time: 15 mins

- ¾ cup milk
- 1 cup flour
- 1 teaspoon cinnamon
- ½ teaspoon baking soda
- 1 egg
- (2) Apple Topping
- ⅓ cup maple syrup
- 1 ½ tablespoons vinegar
- 3 tablespoons sugar
- 1 teaspoon baking powder
- ½ teaspoon salt
- 2 tablespoons oil
- 2 tablespoons butter

1. Preheat a skillet (275 degrees). Whisk the milk and vinegar and leave for 5 minutes.
2. Mix flour, sugar, baking powder, baking soda, and salt in a large bowl. Whisk egg and oil into milk.
3. Add wet ingredients to dry ingredients and stir. Spray skillet with cooking spray.
4. Pour the batter into the skillet and cook for 2 minutes until bubbles form and the edges start to look "dry".
5. Use a spatula to flip the pancake and cook for 2 minutes. Set pancakes aside. Add butter, apples, brown sugar, and cinnamon to saucepan.
6. Stir over medium heat until the apples are very tender. Stir in syrup.

Per Serving: Calories: 405 / Carbs: 73 g / Protein: 7 g / Fat: 10 g / Fiber: 3g

SMASHED AVOCADO AND TOMATO ON TOAST

Serves 4 / Prep time: 10 mins/ Cook time: 15 mins

- 20 Cherry Tomatoes (250g)
- 2 medium-sized Avocados, roughly diced
- 1 heaped tbsp finely diced Fresh Basil
- Extra Virgin Olive Oil.
- 4 small slices of Sourdough, toasted
- 4 tbsp crumbled Feta
- 1 / 2 Lemon, juice only
- Salt & Cracked Black Pepper

1. In a baking dish combine cherry tomatoes with extra virgin olive oil and a pinch of salt and pepper.
2. Heat the oven at 200C / 390F until they begin to lightly wrinkle
3. In a mixing bowl, add avocado, basil, lemon juice, extra virgin olive oil, a pinch of salt and pepper. Smash with a fork, leaving a few lumps.
4. Pour in 4 slices of toast, top with crumbled feta. Add 5 roasted cherry tomatoes to each slice, then drizzle over some of the juices from the baking dish. Enjoy!

Per Serving: Calorie: 317 / Carbs: 22.02 g / Protein: 6.79g / Fat: 24.26g / Fiber: 8.1g

CHOCOLATE CHIP BANANA BREAD

Serves 10 / Prep time:15 mins/ Cook time: 1 hr 10 mins

- 2 cups all-purpose flour
- 1 teaspoon baking soda
- 3 ripe bananas, mashed
- 1 teaspoon ground cinnamon
- ½ cup butter softened
- 1 cup semisweet chocolate chips
- 1 teaspoon baking powder
- 1 teaspoon salt
- 1 tablespoon milk
- 1 cup white sugar
- 2 large eggs

1. Preheat the oven to 165°C. Grease a 9x5-inch loaf pan. Mix flour, baking powder, baking soda, and salt in a bowl.
2. In another bowl, stir bananas, milk, and cinnamon. Beat sugar and butter in another bowl until light and fluffy; add eggs one at a time
3. Stir banana mixture into butter mixture; mix in flour mixture until just blended. Fold in chocolate chips; pour batter into the prepared loaf pan.
4. Bake in the preheated oven until a toothpick inserted into the center comes out clean
5. Cool in the pan for 10 minutes before removing to cool completely before slicing.

Per Serving: Calorie: 378 / Carbs: 58g / Protein: 5g / Fat: 16g / Fiber: 3g

VEGGIE BREAKFAST BOWL WITH QUINOA AND FRIED EGG

Serves 1 / Prep time: 5 mins/ Cook time: 25 mins

- 3/4 cup bok choy
- 3/4 cup enoki mushrooms, sliced
- 1/2 cup quinoa (not cooked)
- 1 garlic cloves, finely minced
- 1/2 teaspoon freshly ground ginger
- 1/2 tablespoon tamari sauce
- 2 tablespoons olive oil
- 1 large egg
- 1/4 cup pea shoots
- Salt and pepper
- Pinch of crushed red pepper flakes

1. Cook quinoa according to package directions. Once quinoa is cooked, add garlic, ginger, and tamari sauce. Cook until fragrant.
2. Heat a large pan with 1 / 2 tbsp oil and saute bok choy and mushrooms until softened. Remove from the pan and wipe clean.
3. Heat 1 tbsp olive oil in the pan. Crack the egg into the pan, add salt, black pepper, and red pepper flakes. Cook for 2-4 minutes
4. Lay down the quinoa. Add the sautéed mushroom bok-choy mixture. Top with the fried egg and pea shoots.

Per Serving: Calorie: 712 / Carbs: 91g / Protein: 33g / Fat: 27g / Fiber: 18g

CRANBERRY ORANGE MUFFINS

Serves 12 / Prep time: 15 mins/ Cook time: 25 mins

- 2 cups flour
- 2 teaspoons baking powder
- ½ teaspoon salt
- 1 cup granulated sugar
- zest of 1 orange
- ½ cup vegetable oil
- ½ cup milk
- 2 large eggs
- ¼ cup orange juice
- 2 teaspoons vanilla extract
- 1½ cups of cranberries

1. Preheat the oven to 400F. Line a 12-cup muffin pan with paper liners.
2. In a bowl, sift together flour, baking powder, and salt. In another bowl, combine sugar and orange zest.
3. Mix the zest into the sugar until it feels like wet sand. Whisk in the vegetable oil, milk, eggs, orange juice, and vanilla
4. Pour the sugar mixture into the flour mixture and stir. Fold in the cranberries. Divide the batter among the paper liners.
5. Bake till a toothpick inserted into the center comes out clean. Let cool for a few minutes in the pan before removing and enjoying.

Per Serving: Calories: 250 / Carbs: 36g / Protein: 4g / Fat: 10g / Fiber: 1g

Chapter II Main Recipes

GRILLED CHICKEN BREAST WITH LEMON AND HERBS

Serves 6 / Prep time: 15 mins / Cool time: 2hr 15 mins
- 6 boneless chicken breast halves (about 1 1 / 2 pounds total)   • ¼ cup olive oil
- 6 cloves garlic, minced
- 1 tablespoon lemon peel, finely shredded
- 2 teaspoons snipped fresh thyme
- 1 teaspoon snipped fresh rosemary
- ¼ teaspoon crushed red pepper
- ¼ teaspoon salt
- ⅛ teaspoon ground black pepper
- 1 Fresh thyme sprigs
- 1 Lemon wedges

1. Place chicken in a resealable plastic bag set in a shallow bowl.
2. For marinade, in a small bowl, combine oil, garlic, lemon peel, thyme, rosemary, crushed red pepper, salt, and black pepper. Pour marinade over chicken.
3. Seal bag; turn to coat chicken. Marinate in the refrigerator for 2 to 4 hours, turning the bag occasionally.
4. Drain chicken, discarding marinade. Place chicken on the rack of an uncovered grill directly over medium coals.
5. Grill for 12 to 15 minutes or until chicken is no longer pink (165 degrees F), turning once halfway through grilling.
6. Garnish with fresh thyme sprigs and lemon wedges.

Per Serving: Calories: 188 / Carbs: 1g / Protein: 26g / Fat: 8g / Fiber: 0 g

SPAGHETTI BOLOGNESE

Serves 6 / Prep time: 25 mins/ Cook time: 1hr 50 mins
- 1 tbsp olive oil
- 4 rashers smoked streaky bacon, finely chopped
- 2 medium onions, finely chopped
- 2 carrots, trimmed and finely chopped
- 2 celery sticks, finely chopped
- 2 garlic cloves finely chopped
- 2-3 sprigs of rosemary leaves picked and finely chopped
- 500g beef mince
- For the bolognese sauce
- 2 x 400g tins plum tomatoes
- small pack of basil leaves picked, ¾ finely chopped and the rest left whole for garnish
- 1 tsp dried oregano
- 2 fresh bay leaves
- 2 tbsp tomato purée
- 1 beef stock cube
- 1 red chili deseeded and finely chopped (optional)
- 125ml red wine
- 6 cherry tomatoes sliced in half
- To season and serve
- 75g parmesan grated, plus extra to serve
- 400g spaghetti
- crusty bread to serve (optional)

1. Put a large saucepan on medium heat and add 1 tbsp olive oil. Add 4 finely chopped bacon rashers and fry for 10 mins until golden and crisp.
2. Reduce the heat and add the 2 onions, 2 carrots, 2 celery sticks, 2 garlic cloves, and the leaves from 2-3 sprigs of rosemary, all finely chopped, then fry for 10 mins. Stir the veg often until it softens.
3. Increase the heat to medium-high, add 500g beef mince, and cook stirring for 3-4 mins until the meat is browned all over.
4. Add 2 tins plum tomatoes, the finely chopped leaves from ¾ small pack basil, 1 tsp dried oregano, 2 bay leaves, 2 tbsp tomato purée, 1 beef stock cube, 1 deseeded and finely chopped red chili (if using), 125ml red wine and 6 halved cherry tomatoes.
5. Stir with a wooden spoon, breaking up the plum tomatoes. Bring to the boil, reduce to a gentle simmer, and cover with a lid. Cook for 1 hr 15 mins stirring occasionally, until you have a rich, thick sauce. Add the 75g grated parmesan, check the seasoning and stir.
6. When the bolognese is nearly finished, cook 400g of spaghetti following the pack instructions.

7. Drain the spaghetti and either stir into the bolognese sauce or serve the sauce on top. Serve with more grated parmesan, the remaining basil leaves, and crusty bread, if you like.

Per Serving: Calorie: 624 / Carbs: 58g / Protein: 35g / Fat: 25g / Fiber: 6 g

TERIYAKI SALMON WITH STEAMED BROCCOLI

Serves 4 / Prep time: 15 mins/ Cook time: 25 mins

- 1 cup white rice
- ¼ cup reduced-sodium soy sauce
- 3 cloves garlic, minced
- 2 tablespoons honey
- 2 ounces broccoli florets, about 2-3 cups
- 1 tablespoon cornstarch
- ¼ cup brown sugar, packed
- 1 tablespoon freshly grated ginger
- 4 5-ounce salmon fillets 1

1. In a large saucepan of 1 1/22 cups water, cook rice according to package instructions; set aside.
2. In a small bowl, whisk together cornstarch and 1/4 cup water; set aside.
3. In a small saucepan over medium heat, add soy sauce, brown sugar, garlic, ginger, honey, and 1 cup water; bring to a simmer. Stir in cornstarch mixture until thickened enough to coat the back of a spoon, about 2 minutes; let cool to room temperature.
4. Preheat oven to 400 degrees F. Lightly coat an 8×8 baking dish with nonstick spray.
5. Place salmon filets along with the soy sauce mixture into the prepared baking dish and bake until the fish flakes easily with a fork, about 14-15 minutes.
6. Place broccoli florets into a steamer or colander set over a pan of boiling water. Cover and steam for 5 mins, or until cooked through and vibrant green.
7. Serve salmon immediately with rice and broccoli.

Per Serving: Calorie: 539 / Carbs: 56g / Protein: 35g / Fat: 23g / Fiber: 10g

BEEF STIR-FRY WITH VEGETABLES

Serves 4 / Prep time: 15 mins/ Cook time: 10 mins

- 2 tablespoons vegetable oil
- 1 ½ cups fresh broccoli florets
- 2 carrots, thinly sliced
- 1 teaspoon minced garlic
- 2 tablespoons sesame seeds, toasted
- 1 pound beef sirloin, cut into 2-inch strips
- 1 red bell pepper, cut into matchsticks
- 1 green onion, chopped
- 2 tablespoons soy sauce

1. Heat vegetable oil in a large wok or skillet over medium-high heat; cook and stir beef until browned 3 to 4 minutes.
2. Move beef to the side of the wok and add broccoli, bell pepper, carrots, green onion, and garlic to the center of the wok. Cook and stir vegetables for 2 minutes.
3. Stir beef into vegetables and season with soy sauce and sesame seeds. Continue to cook and stir until vegetables are tender, about 2 more minutes.

Per Serving: Calorie: 268 / Carbs: 9g / Protein: 23g / Fat: 16g / Fiber: 3g

SHRIMP SCAMPI PASTA

Serves 6 / Prep time: 20 mins/ Cook time: 20 mins

- 1 (16 ounces) package of linguine pasta
- 2 tablespoons extra-virgin olive oil
- 2 cloves garlic, minced
- 1 pound shrimp, peeled and deveined
- ½ cup dry white wine
- 2 tablespoons butter
- ¼ cup finely chopped fresh parsley leaves
- 1 teaspoon extra-virgin olive oil, or to taste.
- 2 tablespoons butter
- 2 shallots, finely diced
- 1 pinch red pepper flakes (Optional)
- 1 pinch kosher salt and freshly ground pepper
- 1 lemon, juiced
- 2 tablespoons extra-virgin olive oil

1. Bring a large pot of salted water to a boil; cook linguine in boiling water until nearly tender, 6 to 8 minutes. Drain.
2. Melt 2 tablespoons butter with 2 tablespoons olive oil in a large skillet over medium heat.

3. Cook and stir shallots, garlic, and red pepper flakes in the hot butter and oil until shallots are translucent, 3 to 4 minutes.
4. Season shrimp with kosher salt and black pepper; add to the skillet and cook until pink, stirring occasionally, 2 to 3 minutes. Remove shrimp from the skillet and keep warm.
5. Pour white wine and lemon juice into the skillet and bring to a boil while scraping the browned bits of food off of the bottom of the skillet with a wooden spoon.
6. Melt 2 tablespoons butter in a skillet, stir 2 tablespoons olive oil into the butter mixture, and bring to a simmer.
7. Toss linguine, shrimp, and parsley in the butter mixture until coated; season with salt and black pepper. Drizzle with 1 teaspoon olive oil to serve. Serve hot and enjoy!
Per Serving: Calorie: 511 / Carbs: 58g / Protein: 22g / Fat: 19g / Fiber: 4g

BBQ PULLED PORK SANDWICHES

Serves: 8 / Prep time: 15 mins/ Cook time: 8hrs
- 3 pounds boneless pork shoulder, pork butt, or pork sirloin roast
- 1 teaspoon salt (I use coarse, kosher salt)
- ½ teaspoon black pepper (I use coarsely ground)
- 2 cups water or low-sodium chicken broth
- 2 tablespoons liquid smoke
- 3 cups BBQ sauce (plus more for serving)
1. Cut the pork roast into large 4-inch pieces Season the pork on all sides with salt and pepper.
2. For a slow cooker, add water or broth and liquid smoke to the slow cooker. Add pork. Cover and cook on low for 8-10 hours or high for 5-6 hours, until the pork is fall-apart tender.
3. For a pressure Cooker, decrease the water / broth to 1 cup. Add the water or broth, pork, and liquid smoke to an electric pressure cooker.
4. Secure the lid, set the valve to seal, and cook on high pressure for 55-60 minutes. Let the pressure naturally release for 10 minutes. Quickly release any remaining pressure.
5. Remove the pork from the slow cooker or pressure cooker and discard most of the remaining liquid.
6. Shred the pork using a couple of forks – it should easily fall apart into pieces.
7. Place the meat back in the slow cooker or pressure cooker. Add the BBQ sauce and heat through.
8. Serve on buns with extra barbecue sauce.
Per Serving: Calorie: 670 / Carbs: 41.2g / Protein: 40.3g / Fat: 39.7g / Fiber: 3g

VEGETARIAN CHICKPEA CURRY

Serves 4 / Prep time: 10 mins/ Cook time: 20 mins
- 2 tablespoons grapeseed oil, or preferred oil
- 4-5 cloves garlic, minced
- 1 tablespoon ginger, grated or minced (fresh, frozen, or paste)
- 1 tablespoon curry powder
- ½ teaspoon crushed red pepper
- 14 ounces diced tomatoes, canned
- 15 ounces chickpeas, canned - rinsed and drained
- ⅓ cup vegetable broth, low sodium (sub with water)
- 2-3 teaspoons agave nectar (or any sweetener)
- ¾ teaspoon salt, more to taste
- 1 ¼ cup full-fat coconut milk, canned (shake the can before use)
- 1 lime, juiced
1. In a large pan, heat oil over medium heat. Add garlic and ginger and sauté for 1 minute until fragrant.
2. Now add the curry powder and red pepper. Sauté until fragrant, about 30-60 seconds.
3. Add diced tomatoes, chickpeas, water/broth, agave, and salt. Simmer for 5-8 minutes to reduce the liquid, soften tomatoes and meld flavors. Stir occasionally.
4. Pour in coconut milk and lightly simmer for 5-8 minutes to reduce and thicken.
5. Remove from heat and stir in the lime juice. Taste for seasoning and add more if needed.
6. Top over rice and serve with naan, lime wedges, and cut cilantro if desired. Enjoy!
Per Serving: Calories: 328 / Carbs: 28g / Protein: 8g / Fat: 12g / Fiber: 7g

MARGHERITA PIZZA

Serves 4 / Prep time: 15 mins/ Cook time: 15 mins

- 1 (14-ounce) can of crushed tomatoes, preferably San Marzano
- 3 medium garlic cloves, minced
- ½ teaspoon sugar
- 2 tablespoons extra-virgin olive oil
- 2 (1-lb) homemade pizza doughs
- ¾ teaspoon salt
- ½ teaspoon freshly ground black pepper
- Flour, for stretching the dough
- 8 oz fresh mozzarella, not packed in water, cubed
- ½ cup freshly grated Parmigiano-Reggiano
- ½ cup roughly chopped fresh basil, lightly packed
- 1 tablespoon cornmeal, for baking

1. In a medium bowl, mix / blend the tomatoes, garlic, salt, sugar, pepper, and oil.
2. Preheat the oven to 500°F and set an oven rack in the bottom position. Dust a 13x18-inch baking sheet with half of the cornmeal.
3. On a flat surface, stretch and press one ball of dough into a 12-inch round. Transfer the dough to the cornmeal-dusted baking sheet, and gently stretch it out again so that it maintains its shape.
4. Spread about ¼ cup + 2 tablespoons of the sauce over the dough, leaving a ½-inch border around the edges.
5. Slide the baking sheet into the oven and bake for 7 minutes, until the crust is partially cooked. Remove from the oven, and scatter half of the mozzarella cubes over the sauce, followed by half of the Parmigiano-Reggiano.
6. Slide the pan back into the oven and cook until the crust is golden brown and the cheese is melted and bubbling, about 4 minutes more.
7. Remove the pizza from the oven and transfer to a cutting board. Sprinkle with the basil and slice. Repeat with the remaining pizza dough and ingredients.

Per Serving: Calories: 734 / Carbs: 80g / Protein: 31g / Fat: 32g / Fiber: 4g

BAKED LEMON GARLIC BUTTER CHICKEN

Serves 4 / Prep time: 5 mins/ Cook time: 40 mins

- 4 tablespoons butter, divided
- 2 tablespoons lemon juice
- 4 (8 ounces) skin-on, bone-in chicken thighs
- salt and ground black pepper to taste
- 4 cloves garlic
- ¼ teaspoon onion powder
- 2 tablespoons fresh parsley, chopped

1. Preheat the oven to 375 degrees F (190 degrees C).
2. Place 3 tablespoons butter in a microwave-safe bowl and heat in a microwave oven until melted.
3. Smash garlic cloves with the side of a chef's knife and add garlic to the warm butter. Stir in lemon juice and onion powder; set aside.
4. Sprinkle both sides of the chicken thighs with salt and pepper. Heat the remaining 1 tablespoon of butter in a medium oven-safe skillet over medium-high heat. Brown chicken, skin-side down, for 3 to 4 minutes.
5. Flip the chicken over and brush the skin with the lemon-butter mixture. Pour the remaining butter mixture into the skillet and remove from heat.
6. Bake in the preheated oven until chicken is no longer pink at the bone and the juices run clear for about 30 minutes. Brush skin every 10 minutes with pan juices.
7. Remove the skillet from the oven and place the chicken on a serving platter. Drizzle chicken with pan juices and garnish with parsley.

Per Serving: Calories: 510 / Carbs: 7g / Protein: 41g / Fat: 34g / Fiber: 0g

EGGPLANT PARMESAN

Serves 10 / Prep time: 25 mins/ Cook time: 35 mins

- 3 large eggplant, peeled and thinly sliced
- 4 cups Italian seasoned bread crumbs
- 1 (16-ounce) package of mozzarella cheese, shredded and divided
- ½ cup grated Parmesan cheese, divided
- 2 large eggs, beaten
- 6 cups spaghetti sauce, divided
- ½ teaspoon dried

1. Preheat the oven to 350 degrees F (175 degrees C).
2. Dip eggplant slices in beaten egg, then in bread crumbs to coat. Place in a single layer on a baking sheet.

3. Bake in the preheated oven for 5 minutes. Flip and bake for 5 more minutes.
4. Spread spaghetti sauce to cover the bottom of a 9x13-inch baking dish. Place a layer of eggplant slices in the sauce. Sprinkle it with mozzarella and Parmesan cheese.
5. Repeat layers with remaining sauce, eggplant, and cheese, ending with a cheese layer. Sprinkle basil on top.
6. Bake in the preheated oven until golden brown, about 35 minutes. Serve hot and enjoy!

Per Serving: Calorie: 487 / Carbs: 62g / Protein: 24g / Fat: 16g / Fiber: 9g

HONEY MUSTARD GLAZED SALMON

Serves 4 / Prep time: 10 mins/ Cook time 10 mins

- 1 1 / 2 to 2 pounds (680g to 900g) salmon fillets
- 3 tablespoons honey mustard (1 1 / 2 tablespoons honey plus 1 1 / 2 tablespoon Dijon mustard)
- 3 cloves garlic, minced (about 3 teaspoons)
- 3 tablespoons extra virgin olive oil (divided into 2 tablespoons and 1 tablespoon)
- 1 tablespoon lemon juice   • 1 tablespoon chopped fresh dill
- Salt to taste

1. Preheat the oven to 400°F.
2. In a small bowl, whisk together the honey mustard, garlic, 2 tablespoons of olive oil, lemon juice, dill, and salt.
3. Line a roasting pan with aluminum foil. Brush the salmon fillets on both sides with olive oil. Place fillets skin-side down
4. Place in the oven and bake at 400°F for 8 to 10 minutes, until just barely cooked through.

Per Serving: Calorie: 609 / Carbs: 4g / Protein: 50g / Fat: 43g / Fiber: 0g

CHICKEN ALFREDO PASTA

Serves 6 / Prep time: 15mins/ Cook time: 20 mins

- 1 large boneless/skinless chicken breast, (or 2 small.) About ¾-1 lb.
- 6 tablespoons salted butter, high-quality   • 3 cloves garlic, minced
- 2 tablespoons all-purpose flour   • 3 cups half cream/half milk
- ¾ cup Parmesan cheese, grated   • ½ cup Romano cheese, grated
- Salt and black pepper, to taste.   • ¾ lb. Fettuccine, see notes
- Fresh parsley, to garnish

1. Cut the chicken in half length to create 2-3 thinner slices. Pat dry and season each side with salt and pepper.
2. Heat olive oil on medium-high heat and add the chicken.
3. Sear on each side for about 4-5 minutes, till golden crust. Set aside and let it rest for 10 minutes, then cut into strips.
4. Boil the pasta according to package instructions, then drain. Prepare the sauce while the pasta boils.
5. Melt the butter in the same skillet that you used to cook the chicken over medium heat. Add the garlic and cook for one minute.
6. Whisk in the flour and cook for 2 minutes, stirring continuously. Add the half in small splashes, stirring continuously.
7. Bring to a gentle bubble. Let it simmer on low heat while the pasta finishes cooking. Stir it occasionally.
8. On low heat, slowly stir the grated cheese into the sauce. Add the drained pasta and toss until well combined. Add the chicken back and toss. Allow it to heat for 2 minutes.

Per Serving: Calorie: 637 / Carbs: 50g / Protein: 31g / Fat: 20g / Fiber: 2g

TOFU STIR-FRY WITH SESAME GINGER SAUCE

Serves 4 / Prep time: / 25 mins/ Cook time: 15 mins

- 1 (14-ounce) package of extra firm tofu   • 1 tablespoon cornstarch
- ½ teaspoon kosher salt   • 3 tablespoons high-heat oil (such as avocado)
- 2 ½ cups green beans, cut into 1-inch pieces   • 1 cup baby carrots, cut lengthwise

- sauce:
- 1 tablespoons sesame oil
- 1 ½ tablespoons minced garlic
- 3 tablespoons soy sauce (or GF tamari)
- 3 tablespoons brown sugar
- 2 tablespoons water
- 1 ½ tablespoon grated ginger
- 1 tablespoons rice vinegar
- ¼ teaspoon red pepper flakes
- 1 tablespoon cornstarch

1. Drain tofu from packaging. Place tofu on a plate with a folded tea towel. Place another tea towel on top followed by another plate and a heavy cast iron skillet or metal cans.
2. Let tofu dry for 20 minutes or up to 1 hour. Then, cut into ¾-1 inch cubes and toss in 1 tablespoon of cornstarch and ½ teaspoon of salt in a zip-top bag until coated.
3. While the tofu is drying, prepare the sauce. Combine sauce ingredients in a blender until completely smooth. Set aside.
4. In a large nonstick skillet over medium-high heat, add 2 tablespoons of oil. Add tofu and let fry for 3-7 minutes. Flip tofu as needed to brown on all sides.
5. Add 2 tablespoons of prepared sauce and allow to cook until the sauce coats the tofu; about 2-3 minutes. When the tofu is caramelized, remove to a plate.
6. Add the remaining tablespoon of oil to the pan, if needed. Toss in veggies and cook for 3-4 minutes, Add tofu back to the skillet.
7. Stir the sauce to combine and pour it in. Stir to coat. Cook for an additional 1-2 minutes or until the tofu soaks up the sauce.
8. Serve warm with rice, quinoa, noodles, cauliflower rice, or on its own.

Per Serving: Calories: 565 / Carbs: 17.2g / Protein: 6.7g / Fat: 54.9g / Fiber: 1.1g

STUFFED BELL PEPPERS WITH GROUND TURKEY AND QUINOA

Serves 4 / Prep time: 30 mins / Cook time: 40 mins

- 4-5 bell peppers
- 1 cup water
- 1 lb ground turkey
- 1 tablespoon Italian seasoning
- ½ cup uncooked quinoa
- ½ cup red onion- chopped
- 1 cup tomato sauce + additional 2-3 tablespoons for topping
- Parmesan Cheese

1. In a small pot, boil add ½ cup of quinoa and 1 cup of water. turn to a low simmer for about 15 minutes
2. While the quinoa is cooking, cut the tops off of each bell pepper and remove all the seeds.
3. Then place the bell peppers on a large plate or microwaveable dish, face down. Cook for 2 minutes to help soften them a bit.
4. In a deep skillet, sauté the ground turkey and red onion. When the turkey has started to brown, add in the cooked quinoa along with tomato sauce and 1 tablespoon of Italian seasoning. Cook the mixture for about 10 minutes.
5. Carefully spoon the mixture into each of the bell peppers. Fill each pepper to the top, and place them into an oven-safe baking dish.
6. Before placing the peppers into the oven, top them with the remaining amount of tomato sauce.
7. Bake for 30-35 minutes at 375 degrees F. Add Parmesan cheese to your peppers, in the last 5 minutes.

Per Serving: Calories: 538 / carbs: 25.4g / Protein: 26.2g / Fat: 34.4g / Fiber: 3.1g

PESTO PASTA WITH CHERRY TOMATOES

Serves 4 / Prep time: 10 mins/ Cook time: 10 mins

- 1 tbsp olive oil
- 4 garlic cloves, finely chopped
- 1 lemon, zested and juiced
- ¾ x 190g jar spinach and ricotta pesto (or green pesto)
- 330g pack cherry tomatoes, halved
- ½ tsp crushed chilies, plus extra to serve (optional)
- 350g dried spaghetti

1. Heat the oil in a frying pan over medium heat. Add the tomatoes, season well, and fry for 4-5 mins, stirring occasionally, until beginning to soften and caramelize.
2. Stir in the garlic, chilies, and lemon zest, reduce the heat to low, and cook for 2-3 mins until fragrant.
3. Meanwhile, bring a large pan of salted water to the boil and cook the spaghetti to pack instructions.

4. Drain, reserving 2 tbsp of the cooking water.
5. Stir the pesto, lemon juice, and reserved cooking water into the pasta, using tongs to toss everything together to coat.
6. Toss through half the tomatoes, then divide between 4 bowls and spoon over the remaining tomatoes. Sprinkle with extra chilies to serve, if you like.

Per Serving: Calorie: 432 / Carbs: 63g / Protein: 14g / Fat: 15g / Fiber: 12 g

BEEF TACOS WITH AVOCADO SALSA

Serves 8 / Prep time: 10 mins/ Cook time: 10 mins

- 454 gm beef, ground
- 8 medium Taco shells (hard or soft)
- 1 / 2 medium Red onion (diced)
- 1 fruit Lime (juiced)
- 1 package Taco seasoning mix, McCormick
- 1 avocado(s) Avocado (diced)
- 1 / 2 medium pepper(s) Red bell pepper (diced)
- Salt and pepper (to taste)

1. Preheat the oven to 350 degrees F.
2. Cook ground beef in a skillet over medium-high heat until browned. Stir in taco seasoning and cook for an additional 2-3 minutes.
3. Arrange taco shells on a baking sheet and bake for 3-4 minutes, until crispy.
4. In a separate bowl, mix diced avocado, red onion, red bell pepper, lime juice, salt, and pepper.
5. Fill taco shells with beef mixture and top with avocado salsa.

Per Serving: Calorie: 285 / Carbs: 14.7g / Protein: 11.6g / Fat: 20.6g / Fiber: 2.8g

MEDITERRANEAN CHICKPEA SALAD

Serves 6 / Prep time: 10 mins/ Cook time: 10 mins

- 1 teaspoon Dijon mustard
- 1 garlic clove minced
- 1 teaspoon sumac
- Black pepper
- 1 lemon juiced
- 1 teaspoon Aleppo pepper
- Kosher salt
- ¼ cup Extra virgin olive oil
- 2 (15-ounce) cans of chickpeas, drained and rinsed
- 1 large English cucumber, chopped
- 2 cups grape tomatoes, halved
- 2 roasted red peppers, seeded and chopped (or a 16-ounce jar of roasted peppers in oil)
- 1 small red onion or 2 shallots, finely chopped
- 1 cup chopped parsley leaves
- ½ cup chopped mint leaves
- 1 avocado, pitted and roughly chopped

1. In a large bowl, whisk together the Dijon, lemon juice, garlic, Aleppo pepper, sumac, and salt and pepper (about ½ teaspoon each).
2. Whisk, and while whisking, drizzle in enough olive oil to make it nicely glossy and well-balanced.
3. Add the chickpeas, cucumbers, tomatoes, roasted bell peppers, onion, parsley, and mint.
4. Toss gently, add the avocado, and toss very gently once more.
5. Enjoy! Taste and adjust the seasoning to your liking and serve immediately.

Per Serving: Calorie: 173 / Carbs: 12g / Protein: 2.5g / Fat: 14.4g / Fiber: 4.9g

LEMON HERB GRILLED SHRIMP SKEWERS

Serves 4 / Prep time: 10 mins/ Cook time: 5 mins

- 1 pound extra large shrimp, peeled and deveined
- Gremolata recipe
- Lemon wedges, if desired

1. Make a gremolata recipe in the bowl of a food processor. Blend until you have a smooth green mixture. Divide the dip in half and set aside.
2. Pour half of the dip over the shrimp and toss to coat. Cover and refrigerate for 30 minutes.
3. Heat grill to medium-high heat (475°F - 500°F // 240°C - 260°C), skewer shrimp and grill for 2 minutes per side. *Set skewers aside to cool slightly.
4. Remove shrimp from skewers, if desired, and serve with the reserved gremolata for dipping and extra lemon.

Per Serving: Calorie: 141 / Carbs: 4g / Protein: 26g / Fat: 1g / Fiber: 1g

CHICKEN AND VEGETABLE KEBABS

Serves 6 / Prep time: 5 mins/ Cook time: 10 mins

- ¼ cup olive oil
- ¼ cup chopped parsley
- 1 lemon, juiced
- To Build the Skewers
- ½ lb chicken (boneless, skinless thighs work best), cut into 1-inch pieces
- 8 oz whole mushrooms, stems removed • 8 oz cherry tomatoes
- 2-3 green onions, cut into 1-inch pieces
- ¼ cup chopped basil
- 2 cloves garlic, minced
- 1 teaspoon salt

1. Combine the ingredients for the marinade in a large bowl or ziplock bag. Add the chicken pieces and thoroughly coat.
2. Cover the bowl or seal the bag and marinate for at least 30 minutes, up to two hours
3. Fire up your grill or get your campfire going. You'll be cooking the kebabs over medium-high to high heat.
4. Build the kabobs by threading the chicken and vegetables onto your skewers.
5. Grill the kabobs over medium-high to high heat, turning occasionally so they cook evenly until the chicken is cooked for 10 minutes total. Remove from grill.

Per Serving: Calorie: 276 / Carbs: 11g / Protein: 26g / Fat: 14g / Fiber: 2g

SPINACH AND FETA STUFFED CHICKEN BREAST

Serves 4 / Prep time: 25 mins/ Cook time: 35 mins

- 1 tablespoon olive oil
- 2 tablespoons chopped fresh dill
- 2 ounces crumbled feta cheese (about 1 / 2 cup)
- 4 (6 ounces) skinless, boneless chicken breasts
- ½ teaspoon kosher salt
- 1 ½ teaspoons olive oil
- 1 cup chopped yellow onion
- 5 ounces baby spinach
- ¼ teaspoon black pepper

1. Heat a large skillet over medium heat. Add 1 tablespoon of olive oil to the pan.
2. Add onion; cook for 8 minutes, stirring frequently. Remove pan from heat; stir in dill, spinach, and feta cheese. Cool for 10 minutes.
3. Cut a horizontal slit through the center of each chicken breast to form a pocket. Stuff each pocket evenly with the spinach mixture.
4. Close pockets with toothpicks. Sprinkle with salt and pepper. Heat skillet over medium-high heat.
5. Add 1 ½ teaspoons of olive oil to the pan. Add chicken; cook for 4 minutes. Turn chicken.
6. Cover the pan, reduce heat to medium, and cook for 5 minutes or until the chicken is done.

Per Serving: Calorie: 319 / Carbs: 2g / Protein: 36g / Fat: 18g / Fiber: 1g

BLACK BEAN AND CORN QUESADILLAS

Serves 8 / Prep time: 10 mins/ Cook time: 30 mins

- 2 teaspoons olive oil
- 21 (15.5 ounce) can black beans, drained and rinsed
- 1 (10 ounces) can whole kernel corn, drained
- ¼ cup salsa
- ¼ teaspoon red pepper flakes
- 8 (8 inch) flour tortillas
- 3 tablespoons finely chopped onion
- 1 tablespoon brown sugar
- 2 tablespoons butter, or as needed
- 1 ½ cups shredded Monterey Jack cheese

1. Heat olive oil in a large saucepan over medium heat. Cook and stir onion in hot oil until softened, about 2 minutes.
2. Stir in beans and corn, then add salsa, brown sugar, and red pepper flakes; mix well.
3. Cook until heated through, about 3 minutes. Remove from heat.
4. Melt about 1 ½ teaspoons butter in a large skillet over medium heat.

5. Place a tortilla in the skillet. Sprinkle it with 1 / 4 of the Monterey Jack cheese, then top with 1 / 4 of the bean mixture.
6. Place another tortilla on top; cook until the bottom is golden, then carefully flip and cook until the other side is golden. Repeat with remaining tortillas and filling.

Per Serving: Calorie: 363 / Carbs: 46g / Protein: 14g / Fat: 7g / Fiber: 6g

ONE-PAN BAKED ZITI

Serves 6 / Prep time: 5 mins/ Cook time: 35 mins

- 1 pound ground Italian sausage
- 8 ounces tomato sauce
- 1 / 4 teaspoon crushed red pepper flakes
- 1 Tablespoon dried basil 1 / 2 teaspoon dried oregano leaves
- 3 cups water
- 1 / 2 cup half and half (or heavy cream)
- freshly ground black pepper
- 14.5-ounce can of diced tomatoes
- 5-6 cloves garlic, minced
- 12 ounces ziti pasta (or similar pasta)
- 1 / 2 cup freshly grated parmesan cheese
- 1 cup shredded mozzarella cheese

1. Preheat oven to 450 degrees F. Heat a large 12-inch or bigger oven-safe skillet over medium heat.
2. Add sausage and cook, crumbling into small pieces, until browned, about 3-5 minutes.
3. Add the garlic and crushed red pepper flakes to the pan and cook for 1-2 minutes.
4. Add the diced tomatoes, tomato sauce, dried basil and oregano. Stir well. Reduce heat and simmer, stirring occasionally, for 5-10 minutes.
5. Add the water and dry pasta. Boil, cover, reduce heat to low, and cook, stirring occasionally, for 10-15 minutes or until noodles are tender.
6. Stir in the half and half, and parmesan cheese and season with salt and pepper to taste. Sprinkle mozzarella evenly on top.
7. Transfer the skillet to the oven and bake until the cheese has melted and browned, about 5 minutes. Enjoy!

Per Serving: Calorie: 548 / Carbs: 52g / Protein: 27g / Fat: 30g / Fiber: 3g

THAI BASIL BEEF STIR-FRY

Serves 5 / Prep time: 10 mins/ Cook time: 20 mins

- 2 Tablespoons vegetable oil
- 8 cloves garlic, minced
- 1 red bell pepper, thinly sliced
- 1 Tablespoon brown sugar
- 1 / 2 cup low-sodium soy sauce
- 2 or 3 Tablespoons chili paste with garlic*
- 1 / 3 cup water
- 1.5 cups holy basil leaves*, chopped
- 5 cups hot cooked rice
- 2 shallots, chopped
- 1 Tablespoon fresh ginger, minced
- 1.5 lbs lean ground beef*
- 1 Tablespoon fish sauce
- 1.5 Tablespoons oyster sauce*
- 3 / 4 cup low-sodium beef broth
- 2 teaspoons cornstarch
- 3 green onions chopped, for garnish

1. In a large skillet over medium-high heat, add the oil, shallots, garlic, ginger, and bell peppers and sauté for 2-3 minutes.
2. Push the veggies off to the side and add the ground beef, breaking it up into small pieces as it cooks.
3. In a small bowl, stir together the brown sugar, fish sauce, soy sauce, oyster sauce, chili paste, cornstarch, beef broth, and water, and add to the pan.
4. Simmer for 5-10 minutes. Add the basil and stir. Serve over hot steamed rice, with chopped green onion on top.

Per Serving: Calorie: 25 / Carbs: 11g / Protein:34g / Fat: 13g / Fiber: 1g

CAPRESE STUFFED PORTOBELLO MUSHROOMS

Serves 4 / Prep time: 20 mins/ Cook time: 15 mins

- 3 tablespoons extra-virgin olive oil, divided
- ½ teaspoon salt, divided
- 1 medium clove garlic, minced
- ½ teaspoon ground pepper, divided

- 4 portobello mushrooms (about 14 ounces), stems and gills removed
- 1 cup halved cherry tomatoes
- ½ cup fresh mozzarella pearls drained and patted dry
- ½ cup thinly sliced fresh basil
- 2 teaspoons of best-quality balsamic vinegar
1. Preheat oven to 400 degrees F.
2. Mix 2 tablespoons oil, garlic, 1 / 4 teaspoon salt, and 1 / 4 teaspoon pepper in a small bowl.
3. Using a silicone brush, coat mushrooms all over with the oil mixture. Place on a large rimmed baking sheet and bake until the mushrooms are mostly soft for about 10 minutes.
4. Meanwhile, stir tomatoes, mozzarella, basil, and the remaining 1 / 4 teaspoon salt, 1 / 4 teaspoon pepper, and 1 tablespoon oil together in a medium bowl.
5. Once the mushrooms have softened, remove from the oven and fill with the tomato mixture.
6. Bake until the cheese is fully melted and the tomatoes have wilted, about 12 to 15 minutes more. Drizzle each mushroom with 1 / 2 teaspoon vinegar and serve.

Per Serving: Calorie: 186 / Carbs: 6g / Protein: 6g / Fat: 16g / Fiber: 2g

BUTTERNUT SQUASH RISOTTO

Serves 4 / Prep time: 10 mins/ Cook time: 40 mins

- 1kg butternut squash, peeled and cut into bite-size chunks
- 3 tbsp olive oil
- bunch of sage, leaves picked, half roughly chopped, half left whole
- 1½l vegetable stock
- 50g butter
- 1 onion, finely chopped
- 300g risotto rice (we used arborio)
- 1 small glass of white wine
- 50g parmesan or vegetarian alternative, finely grated
1. Heat the oven to 220C / 200C. Toss the squash in 1 tbsp oil together with the chopped sage. Scatter into a shallow roasting tin and roast for 30 minutes until brown and soft.
2. While the squash is roasting, prepare the risotto. Bring the stock to the boil and keep on a low simmer.
3. In a separate pan, melt half the butter over a medium heat. Stir in the onions and cook gently for 8-10 mins until soft but not colored, stirring occasionally.
4. Stir the rice into the onions until completely coated in the butter, then stir continuously until the rice is shiny and the edges of the grain start to look transparent.
5. Pour the wine and simmer until completely evaporated. Add the stock, in bits and stir the rice over low heat for 30 mins, until the rice is cooked. The risotto should be creamy.
6. At the same time, gently fry the whole sage leaves in a little olive oil until crisp, then set aside on kitchen paper.
7. When the squash is cooked, mash half of it to a rough purée and leave half whole. When the risotto is done, stir the purée, add the cheese and remaining butter; and leave to rest for a few minutes.
8. Serve the risotto scattered with the whole chunks of squash and the crisp sage leaves.

Per Serving: Calorie: 609 / Carbs: 87g / Protein: 15g / Fat:24g / Fiber: 8 g

Chapter III   Fish and Seafood Recipes

COCONUT-CRUSTED TILAPIA

Serves 4 / Prep time: 10 mins/ Cook time: 15 mins

- 4 (6 ounce) tilapia fillets
- 1 cup shredded coconut
- 2 teaspoons cumin
- ½ teaspoon powdered garlic
- ½ teaspoon turmeric
- 1 (14-ounce) can of coconut milk
- 1 teaspoon kosher salt
- 1 teaspoon paprika
- ½ teaspoon ground ginger
- ¼ teaspoon cayenne

1. Preheat the oven to 400 degrees F. Cover the tilapia in the coconut milk and let it marinate in the refrigerator for at least 10 minutes.
2. Combine the coconut, cumin, paprika, garlic, ginger, turmeric, and cayenne. Spread the coconut mixture across a plate.
3. Remove the tilapia from the refrigerator and sprinkle with that salt. Then coat each side with the coconut mixture.
4. Place fillets on a parchment-lined baking sheet and bake the tilapia for 15 minutes or until the fish is flaky. Serve immediately

Per Serving: Calorie: 351 / Carbs: 13g / Protein: 46g / Fat: 0g / Fiber: 3g

CAJUN SHRIMP PASTA

Serves 6 / Prep time: 5mins/ Cook time: 20 mins

- 8 oz penne pasta
- 1 Tbsp olive oil
- 2 Tbsp unsalted butter
- 1 / 2 cup diced tomatoes
- 1 / 2 cup grated parmesan cheese, plus more to serve
- 2 Tbsp parsley to garnish, (optional)
- 1 lb large shrimp, peeled and deveined
- 2 Tbsp cajun seasoning, divided
- 2 garlic cloves, minced
- 1 1 / 2 cups heavy whipping cream

1. Cook the penne pasta in a pot of salted water until al dente according to package instructions. Drain the water and cover the pasta to keep warm.
2. Coat the shrimp with 1 Tbsp of the cajun seasoning. In a deep skillet, heat 1 Tbsp oil over medium heat.
3. Once hot, add the seasoned shrimp in a single layer and saute for about 1-2 minutes per side, remove from the skillet and cover to keep warm.
4. In the same skillet, melt 2 Tbsp butter with the minced garlic and cook for 30 seconds until fragrant. Add in the diced tomatoes and saute for about 2-3 minutes.
5. Pour in the heavy whipping cream, remaining 1 Tbsp cajun seasoning, and grated parmesan cheese.
6. Bring to a simmer then reduce to medium / low heat and continue for 2-3 minutes or until the sauce thickens.
7. Add the shrimp and pasta back into the skillet and stir until the noodles are coated in sauce and everything is heated through. Garnish with chopped parsley and serve.

Per Serving: Calorie: 523 / Carbs: 33g / Protein: 25g / Fat: 32g / Fiber: 2g

GRILLED SWORDFISH WITH LEMON-DILL SAUCE

Serves 4 / Prep time: 10 mins/ Cook time: 10 mins

- 4 swordfish steaks, about 1 / 2 inch thick
- 1/2 cup unsalted butter
- 1/4 cup dry white wine
- 1 tablespoon cornstarch
- 6 sprigs fresh dill, minced
- 1 lemon, juice of
- fresh ground pepper

1. Season swordfish with pepper and broil for 5 minutes on each side. Remove and keep warm.

2. In a medium skillet over medium heat, melt butter. Add lemon juice white wine and dill. Season with pepper to taste.
3. Remove some of the liquid and let it cool. Add the cornstarch to the cooled liquid and mix until smooth.
4. Add this back into skillet and simmer, stirring until slightly thickened.
5. Remove swordfish steaks and place them on plates. Spoon sauce over each steak and garnish with dill sprigs.

Per Serving: Calorie: 314 / Carbs: 42g / Protein: 20g / Fat: 15g / Fiber: 3g

TUNA SALAD LETTUCE WRAPS

Serves 2 / Prep time: 10 mins

- 2 cans tuna in water
- ⅓ cup celery, finely chopped
- 2 tablespoons pickle relish
- 1 teaspoon whole-grain mustard
- 1 tablespoon fresh lemon juice
- pepper, to taste
- ⅓ cup mayonnaise
- ¼ cup red onion, finely chopped
- 1 tablespoon capers
- 2 tablespoons fresh parsley, chopped
- salt, to taste
- 6 butter lettuce leaves, rinsed and patted dry

1. Add the tuna, mayonnaise, celery, red onion, pickle relish, capers, whole grain mustard, parsley, and lemon juice to a mixing bowl.
2. Mix the ingredients thoroughly. Season with salt and pepper to taste. Serve the tuna salad in the lettuce leaves. Garnish as desired.

Per Serving: Calorie: 448 / Carbs: 9.6g / Protein: 33.1 / Fat: 31 / 6 / Fiber: 1.5g

CRAB CAKES WITH REMOULADE SAUCE

Serves 8 / Prep time: 20 mins/ Cook time: 8 mins

- 1 lb lump crab meat
- 1 tsp old bay seasoning or Cajun seasoning
- 1 / 2 tbsp Dijon mustard
- 1 / 2 tbsp lemon juice
- 1 / 4 tsp lemon zest
- 1 tbsp lemon juice
- 1 garlic clove
- 1 tsp paprika
- 2 tbsp capers
- It has 10 saltine crackers
- m1 / 4 cup mayo
- 1 egg
- 1 / 4 tsp Worcestershire sauce
- m1 / 2 cup mayo
- 1 / 2 onion
- 2 tsp Dijon mustard
- 1 tbsp sriracha sauce
- salt and pepper to taste

1. Place the saltine crackers in a food processor and blend until fine crumbs.
2. In a large bowl, mix the egg, mayo, Worcestershire sauce, lemon juice, lemon zest, old bay seasoning, dijon mustard, and saltine crackers. Mix well.
3. Fold in the crab meat gently and mix until well combined. Cover and refrigerate for one hour.
4. Tightly form the crab cakes and place them on a baking sheet. Refrigerate for 10-15 minutes.
5. Add some oil to a non-stick skillet and heat over medium-high heat. Fry the crab cakes for 3-4 minutes on each side.
6. To make the remoulade sauce, place all of the remoulade ingredients in a food processor minus the capers and blend until smooth. Season with salt and pepper and stir in the capers.
7. Enjoy the crab cakes with the remoulade sauce and fresh lemon.

Per Serving: Calorie: 222 / Carbs:4g / Protein: 12g / Fat: 17g / Fiber: 1g

BAKED COD WITH GARLIC AND HERB BUTTER

Serves 2 / Prep time: 10 mins/ Cook time: 10 mins

- 4 (6-ounce) cod filets
- 1 tablespoon extra virgin olive oil
- 2 tablespoons parsley, chives, thyme or other herbs, finely chopped
- ½ teaspoon paprika
- kosher salt and freshly ground black pepper, to taste
- 3 tablespoons butter, softened
- 3 garlic cloves, minced
- 1 lemon, thinly sliced

1. Preheat your oven to 400°F (200°C). Place the cod in a baking dish.
2. In a small bowl, mix the butter, olive oil, minced garlic, parsley, paprika, salt, and pepper. Spread the compound butter mixture on top of each filet.
3. Bake in the oven for 13 to 15 minutes, or until the cod is opaque and flakes easily with a fork. Before serving, spoon the juices from the baking dish over the cod.

Per Serving: Calorie: 258 / Carbs: 4g / Protein: 31g / Fat: 6g / Fiber: 1g

LEMON BUTTER GARLIC SHRIMP

Serves 4 / Prep time: 10 mins/ Cook time: 10 mins

- 1 / 3 cup butter, divided
- 4 cloves garlic, minced (or 1 tablespoon)
- 1 3 / 4 pounds (800 g) shrimp (or prawns), peeled and deveined, tails intact
- Kosher salt and freshly ground black pepper, to taste
- Juice of half a lemon (about 2 tablespoons -- add more if desired)
- 2 tablespoons water
- Fresh chopped parsley, to garnish

1. Melt 2 tablespoon butter in a large skillet over medium-high heat. Add the garlic and cook until fragrant (about 1 minute).
2. Fry shrimp and add salt and pepper to your taste. Cook for 2 minutes on one side, while stirring occasionally.
3. Flip and cook for 2 minutes on the other side until JUST beginning to turn pink.
4. Add in the remaining butter, lemon juice, and water. Cook, while stirring, until the butter melts and the shrimp have cooked.
5. Take off the heat. Taste test, and add more lemon juice, salt, or pepper, if needed to suit your tastes.
6. Garnish with fresh chopped parsley and serve over rice or pasta.

Per Serving: Calorie: 338 / Carbs: 1g / Protein: 40g / Fat: 18g / Fiber: 0g

SEARED AHI TUNA WITH SOY GINGER GLAZE

Serves 2 / Prep time: 20 mins/ Cook time: 5 mins

- 1 tablespoon fresh lime juice
- 2 teaspoons sesame oil
- 2 6 ounces each sushi-grade ahi tuna steaks, about 1 inch each
- ½ teaspoon ground pepper
- 2 tablespoons soy sauce
- 1 1-inch piece fresh ginger, sliced
- 1 green onion thinly sliced

1. In a small bowl, whisk together the fresh lime juice, soy sauce, and sesame oil.
2. Pour the mixture into a large resealable plastic bag. Add the ginger slices.
3. Season the ahi tuna steaks with pepper, transfer to the bag seal the bag, and marinate for 15 minutes.
4. Transfer the marinade to a medium glass bowl and microwave for 1 minute. Heat a nonstick skillet, cast iron skillet, or grill pan over medium-high heat.
5. Sear the fish until the desired degree of doneness is reached, about 2 minutes per side.
6. Thinly slice the ahi. Garnish with green onions and serve with the heated marinade.

Per Serving: Calorie: 232 / Carbs: 7.7g / Protein: 38g / Fat: 0.6g / Fiber: 0.4g

FISH TACOS WITH MANGO SALSA

Serves 8 / Prep time: 20 mins/ Cook time: 15 mins

- 1 mango - peeled, seeded, and chopped
- 1 cup chopped tomato
- ½ cup diced red pepper
- 2 tablespoons canola oil
- 1 lime, juiced
- 1 dash of hot pepper sauce, or to taste
- 8 taco shells
- 1 teaspoon ground black pepper
- 2 avocados - peeled, pitted, and chopped
- ½ cup diced red onion
- 2 tablespoons chopped fresh flat-leaf parsley
- 2 tablespoons brown sugar
- 1 teaspoon cider vinegar
- Salt and ground black pepper to taste
- 4 (6 ounces) mahi mahi fillets, cut into 1-inch slices
- 1 teaspoon paprika

- ½ teaspoon salt
- 2 tablespoons olive oil

1. Stir mango, avocado, tomato, red onion, red pepper, parsley, canola oil, brown sugar, lime juice, cider vinegar, hot pepper sauce, salt, and ground black pepper together in a bowl. Refrigerate salsa for at least 1 hour.
2. Preheat the oven to 325 degrees F (165 degrees C). Heat taco shells in a preheated oven until crisp, about 5 minutes.
3. Season mahi mahi with 1 teaspoon ground black pepper, paprika, and 1 / 2 teaspoon salt.
4. Heat olive oil in a skillet over medium-high heat. Cook mahi mahi in olive oil until the fish flakes easily, about 3 minutes per side.
5. Place mahi mahi slices in taco shells and top with mango salsa.

Per Serving: Calorie: 324 / Carbs: 24g / Protein: 19g / Fat: 18g / Fiber: 6g

BAKED LEMON PEPPER SALMON

Serves 6 / Prep time: 10 mins/ Cook time: 15 mins

- 2-pound side of salmon boneless
- 2 medium lemons plus additional for serving
- 1 teaspoon kosher salt
- 1 / 2 teaspoon freshly ground black pepper plus additional to taste
- finely chopped fresh herbs of choice (I prefer parsley or basil)
- 10 sprigs of fresh thyme optional
- 2 tablespoons extra virgin olive oil

1. Remove the salmon from the refrigerator, and wait for 10 minutes while you prepare the other ingredients. Heat oven to 375 degrees F.
2. Line a rimmed baking sheet large enough to hold your piece of salmon with a large piece of aluminum foil, lightly coat the foil with baking spray, then arrange 5 sprigs of the thyme down the middle.
3. Cut one of the lemons into thin slices and arrange half of the slices down the middle too. Place the salmon on top. Drizzle the salmon with the olive oil.
4. Zest the second lemon over the salmon and sprinkle with the salt and pepper. Lay the remaining thyme and lemon slices on top of the salmon. Juice the zested lemon, then pour the juice over the top.
5. Fold the sides of the aluminum foil up and over the top of the salmon until it is completely enclosed. Leave a little room inside the foil for air to circulate.
6. Bake the salmon for 18-21 minutes, until the salmon is almost completely cooked through. The cooking time depends on the thickness of your salmon.
7. Remove the salmon from the oven, and carefully open the foil so that the top of the fish is completely uncovered.
8. Change the oven setting to broil, then return the fish to the oven and broil for 3 minutes, until the top of the salmon is slightly golden and the fish is cooked through completely.
9. Remove the salmon from the oven. As soon as it flakes easily with a fork, it's ready. Cut the salmon into portions. Sprinkle with additional fresh herbs or top with an extra squeeze of lemon as desired.

Per Serving: Calorie: 268 / Carbs: 10g / Protein: 41g / Fat: 14g / Fiber: 1g

GARLIC PARMESAN BAKED SHRIMP

Serves 4 / Prep time: 10 mins/ Cook time: 15 mins

- 1 pound uncooked medium shrimp, peeled and deveined
- ¼ cup grated Parmesan cheese
- 2 tablespoons olive oil
- ¼ cup melted butter
- 4 cloves garlic, minced
- ½ cup panko bread crumbs

1. Preheat the oven to 425 degrees F (220 degrees C). Combine shrimp, butter, Parmesan cheese, garlic, and oil in a bowl.
2. Stir to combine; pour into a baking dish, spreading out evenly. Top with panko bread crumbs.
3. Bake in the preheated oven until shrimp are bright pink, 15 to 18 minutes.

Per Serving: Calorie: 309 / Carbs: 11g / Protein: 21g / Fat: 22g / Fiber: 0g

SHRIMP AND ASPARAGUS STIR-FRY

Serves 4 / Prep time: 15 mins/ Cook time: 10 mins

- 1 / 4 cup chicken broth
- 2 tablespoons soy sauce
- 1 teaspoon lemon zest
- 2 tablespoons peanut oil, divided
- 1 pound asparagus spears, trimmed and cut into bite-sized pieces
- 1 white onion, cut into 1 / 4-inch wide wedges
- salt and freshly ground black pepper to taste
- lemon slices for garnish (optional)
- 1 / 4 cup lemon juice
- 2 tablespoons brown sugar
- 1 teaspoon cornstarch
- 1 pound large shrimp
- crushed red chilies (optional)

1. Whisk chicken broth, lemon juice, soy sauce, brown sugar, lemon zest, and cornstarch together in a bowl and set aside.
2. Heat 1 tablespoon of oil in a wok or large skillet over medium-high heat. Add asparagus and onion and cook until asparagus is tender-crisp, stirring frequently, 4 to 5 minutes. Remove vegetables from the skillet and set aside.
3. Heat remaining oil in the same skillet over medium-high heat and cook shrimp for 2 minutes, flipping over halfway through.
4. Add asparagus and onion back to the skillet. Stir the sauce and pour over the shrimp. Bring sauce to a simmer, stirring constantly until it thickens, 1 to 2 minutes.
5. Season with salt and pepper, to taste. Garnish with crushed red chilies and lemon slices if desired.

Per Serving: Calorie: 265 / Carbs: 17g / Protein: 30g / Fat: 9g / Fiber: 3g

MAHI-MAHI TACOS WITH CABBAGE SLAW

Serves: 8 / Prep time: 15mins/ Cook time: 20 mins

- 10 to 16 ounces mahi mahi fillets
- 2 tsp chili powder
- Carrot Coleslaw
- 1 avocado
- ¼ cup cilantro
- 1 small clove garlic
- 2 Tbsp avocado oil
- 6 corn tortillas
- Avocado Crema
- ¼ cup plain Greek yogurt or sour cream
- 2 Tbsp fresh lime juice
- ½ tsp sea salt

1. Prepare your coleslaw and set aside. Transfer the mahi mahi, avocado oil, chili powder, and sea salt to a large zip-lock bag.
2. Seal the bag and shake everything together until the fish is coated in oil and seasonings. Marinate for at least 15 minutes, or up to 12 hours.
3. When you're ready to bake the fish, preheat the oven to 400 degrees F. Transfer the marinated fish filets to a casserole dish or baking sheet that is lightly sprayed with cooking spray. Bake for 12 to 15 minutes,
4. To verify it's done, insert a meat thermometer into the thickest part of each filet and wait until the numbers stop moving.
5. Remove the fish from the oven and use a fork to chop it up into chunks. For richer flavor, drizzle the chopped fish with more avocado oil.
6. Add the ingredients for the avocado crema to a small blender. Blend until completely smooth.
7. Heat your tortillas using your preferred method. Stuff the corn tortillas with your desired amount of baked mahi mahi.
8. Top with avocado crema and cabbage slaw. Serve with lime wedges so you can squirt a squeeze of lime juice over the tacos.

Per Serving: Calorie: 241 Carbs: 15 / Protein:17 / Fat10 / Fiber 5

MEDITERRANEAN GRILLED OCTOPUS

Serves 4 / Prep time: 1hr/ Cook time: 1 hr

- 2 lb fresh or frozen octopus
- 2 cloves garlic, thinly sliced
- 1 sprig of fresh thyme
- 1 / 2 cup olive oil
- 1 tbsp dried oregano
- 5 allspice berries
- 2 bay leaves
- 1 / 4 cup balsamic vinegar
- 1 / 2 cup balsamic vinegar
- 1 1 / 2 tbsp freshly squeezed lemon juice

- 1 tbsp finely chopped capers
- 1 teaspoon fresh thyme, finely chopped
- 1 / 4 teaspoon ground black pepper
- 1 garlic clove, thinly sliced
- 1 tbsp flat leaf parsley, finely chopped
- 1 / 2 teaspoon salt

1. If you are using frozen octopus, defrost it completely in the fridge overnight. Rinse your octopus well under cool running water.
2. Place your octopus in a large pot. Add the allspice berries, garlic, bay leaves, and fresh thyme. Add enough water to just cover the octopus.
3. 5 allspice berries, 2 cloves garlic, thinly sliced, 2 bay leaves, and 1 spring of fresh thyme
4. Bring to a boil and then reduce the heat to medium. Cook, covered, for approximately 30 – 40 minutes.
5. The octopus is done when the skirt (the part of the octopus that connects the legs to the head) can easily be pierced by a sharp knife.
6. Remove from the heat and add 1 / 4 cup balsamic vinegar to the cooking liquid. Allow the octopus to steep in this liquid until it comes to room temperature.

Per Serving: Calorie: 439 / Carbs: 5g / Protein: 34g / Fat: 31g / 0.1g

SHRIMP AND AVOCADO SALAD

Serves 4 / Prep time: 20 mins/ Cook time: 20 mins

- 1 cup cooked salad shrimp
- ⅓ cup mayonnaise
- 2 tablespoons chili sauce
- 2 avocados, halved lengthwise and pitted
- Bibb lettuce leaves
- sliced pimento peppers, for garnish
- 2 tablespoons chopped fresh chives
- 1 tablespoon Worcestershire sauce
- salt to taste
- 1 tablespoon lemon juice
- 1 teaspoon paprika

1. In a bowl, mix the shrimp, chives, mayonnaise, Worcestershire sauce, and chili sauce. Season with salt.
2. Mound the shrimp mixture into avocado halves, and sprinkle with lemon juice.
3. Place avocado halves on Bibb lettuce leaves that have been dusted with paprika. Garnish with strips of pimento to serve.

Per Serving: Calorie: 341kcal / Carbs: 14g / Protein: 10g / Fat: 30g / Fiber: 8g

BLACKENED CATFISH WITH CAJUN CREAM SAUCE

Serves 5 / Prep time: 5 mins/ Cook time: 35 mins

- 2 Catfish Fillets
- 8 oz of crawfish tails
- 1 tbsp of flour
- 16 oz of Heavy cream
- 1 cup of Monterey cheese
- Blackened seasoning blend 1/2 tbsp of olive oil
- 1 tbsp of butter
- 1/3 of a yellow onion chopped 1 tbsp of garlic
- 4 oz of Cream cheese
- 1/2 cup of pepper jack cheese

1. Heat olive oil in a skillet over medium-high heat. Season both sides of the catfish with the blackened seasoning.
2. Place fish in the skillet, and cook on both sides for about three minutes. Remove from the skillet and place on a paper towel.
3. Melt butter in a saucepan over medium heat. Add in chopped onions, and saute until nearly translucent.
4. Add in garlic, and when fragrant, stir in the flour for about 2 minutes, then add in the heavy cream.
5. Raise heat to medium-high until it is slightly boiling. Add in the cream cheese and stir until the cream cheese is melted.
6. Season with toms, garlic powder, onion powder, and old bay. About 1/2 tbsp of each.
7. Add in the Monterey and pepper jack cheese. Stir until melted. Reduce heat to medium-low and stir in crawfish tails.
8. Remove from heat and let sit for about 2 minutes. Garnish with parsley, chives, and green onions, and serve!

Per Serving: Calorie: 79 / Carbs: 4g / Protein: 2g / Fat: 9g / Fiber: 1g

GRILLED HALIBUT WITH TOMATO AND HERB SALSA

Serves 4 / Prep time: 25 mins/ Cook time: 30 mins

- 1 lb halibut fillet
- 1 tbsp extra virgin olive oil
- salt, to taste
- ½ cup tomatoes, diced
- 2 tbsp scallions, finely chopped
- 1 tsp extra virgin olive oil
- 1 pinch cayenne pepper, if desired
- 2 tbsp fresh lemon juice
- 1 tsp dried rosemary, crushed
- freshly ground black pepper, to taste
- ¼ cup fresh basil, coarsely chopped
- 1 tbsp red wine vinegar
- ½ tsp orange rind, grated
- fresh rosemary, (optional)

1. In a bowl, mix oil, vinegar, garlic, salt and pepper, then mix. After this, add the tomatoes and basil. Stir to combine gently. Set aside.
2. Preheat your grill to medium-high in preparation fpr the fish. Season the fish wih salt and pepper, (and other condiments, then wrap in foil.
3. Place the fish on the grill, foil side down and cook until the fish flakes with a fork,
4. Stir the salsa, then drizzle over the fish. Serve immediately.

Per Serving: Calorie: 152 / Carbs: 2g / Protein: 21g / Fat: 6g / Fiber: 1g

LOBSTER MAC AND CHEESE

Serves 6 / Prep time: 20 mins/ Cook time: 40 mins

- 8 ounces lobster meat cooked, chopped, about 2 cups *see note
- 16 ounces dry pasta cavatappi, penne, or shells
- ⅓ cup flour
- ½ teaspoon dry mustard powder
- ¼ teaspoon Old Bay Seasoning
- 2 ¾ cups milk
- 2 cups sharp cheddar shredded
- ⅓ cup butter
- 1 teaspoon onion powder
- ½ teaspoon salt or to taste
- ¼ teaspoon black pepper to taste
- ½ cup light cream
- 1 teaspoon parsley chopped
- 1 ¼ cups Gruyere cheese shredded, or Swiss cheese, mozzarella, or Havarti
- ½ cup fresh parmesan cheese shredded
- 2 tablespoons butter melted
- ½ cup bread crumbs
- 2 tablespoons parmesan cheese grated

1. Preheat oven to 400°F. Grease a 9x13 pan. Combine the topping ingredients in a small bowl. Set aside.
2. Cook pasta al dente according to package directions. Drain and run under cold water and set aside.
3. While pasta is cooking, melt butter over medium heat in a saucepan. Stir in flour and seasonings and cook for 2 minutes.
4. Combine milk and cream. Add to the flour mixture a little bit at a time whisking in after each addition. The mixture will smooth out as you continue adding liquid.
5. Once all of the liquid is added, bring the mixture to a boil. Reduce heat and simmer for 1-2 minutes or until thickened while whisking.
6. Remove from heat and stir in the cheeses whisking until the sauce is smooth and melted. Combine the sauce and the pasta.
7. Gently stir in half of the lobster meat and spread into the prepared pan. Add the remaining lobster meat on top and sprinkle with the topping mixture. Bake for 20-25 minutes or until bubbly and topping is browned. Do not overcook

Per Serving: Calorie: 887 / Carbs: 75g / Protein: 45g / Fats: 45g / Fiber / 3g

SMOKED SALMON AND CREAM CHEESE BAGEL

Serves: 2 / Prep time:10 mins/ Cook time: 10 mins

- 2 bagels halved
- 4 ounces cream cheese
- 1 tablespoon fresh dill plus more for serving
- 1-2 Persian cucumbers peeled in ribbons
- Capers to taste
- 4 ounces smoked salmon thinly sliced
- 2 tablespoons lemon juice
- Salt and pepper to taste
- Red onion slices for serving

1. In a small bowl, combine the cream cheese, lemon juice, fresh dill, and salt and pepper, to taste.
2. Toast the bagels, then spread the cream cheese mixture on both sides of the bagel.
3. Add the cucumbers, smoked salmon, capers, and red onions to the bottom of the toasted bagels. Top with the top of the bagels.

Per Serving: Calorie: 577 / Carbs: 64g / Protein: 26g / Fat: 24g / Fiber: 4g

SHRIMP AND GRITS

Serves 4 / Prep time: 15 mins/ Cook time: 25

- 4 cups water
- 1 cup stone-ground grits
- 2 cups shredded sharp cheddar cheese
- 6 slices bacon, chopped
- 2 tablespoons chopped parsley
- 1 large clove garlic, minced
- Salt and pepper
- 3 tablespoons butter
- 1 pound shrimp, peeled and deveined
- 4 teaspoons lemon juice
- 1 cup thinly sliced scallions

1. Bring water to a boil. Add salt and pepper. Add grits and cook until water is absorbed about 20 to 25 minutes. Remove from heat and stir in butter and cheese.
2. Rinse shrimp and pat dry. Fry the bacon in a large skillet until browned; drain well. In grease, add shrimp.
3. Cook until the shrimp turn pink. Add lemon juice, chopped bacon, parsley, scallions, and garlic. Saute for 3 minutes.
4. Spoon grits into a serving bowl. Add shrimp mixture and mix well. Serve immediately.

Per Serving: Calorie: 782 / Carbs: 36g / Protein: 48g / Fat: 50g / Fiber: 3g

BAKED TERIYAKI GLAZED SALMON

Serves 8 / Prep time: 25 mins/ Cook time: 15 mins

- 2 1 / 2 lbs salmon filet sliced into 2" wide slices
- 3 Tbsp hoisin sauce
- 1 Tbsp white vinegar
- 1 / 3 cup packed light brown sugar
- 2 tsp freshly grated ginger, or 1 / 2 tsp ground ginger
- Sesame seeds to garnish, optional
- 3 Tbsp teriyaki sauce
- 3 Tbsp soy sauce
- 1 Tbsp sesame oil
- 2 large or 3 medium garlic cloves, minced
- Green onion, chopped, optional

1. Combine sauce ingredients and stir until brown sugar is dissolved.
2. Place individual salmon slices in a mixing bowl. Pour the sauce over the salmon, cover with plastic wrap, and let marinate for 20 minutes
3. Transfer salmon to a prepared baking sheet (keep the marinade). Bake at 400 until salmon is flaky and cooked through.
4. While salmon is baking, transfer the remaining marinade to a small saucepan and bring to a boil then reduce heat to a simmer and cook, stirring occasionally until slightly thickened then remove from heat.
5. Once the salmon is out of the oven, brush with teriyaki syrup, then sprinkle with chopped green onion and sesame seeds as desired.

Per Serving: Calorie: 279 / Carbs: 13g / Protein: 29g / Fat: 10g

THAI COCONUT CURRY MUSSELS

Serves 6 / Prep time: 20 mins/ Cook time: 10mins

- 1 (13.5 ounces) can of unsweetened coconut milk
- ⅓ cup dry white wine
- 1 ½ tablespoons minced garlic
- 1 tablespoon white sugar
- 2 cups chopped fresh cilantro
- ⅓ cup fresh lime juice
- 1 ½ tablespoons Thai red curry paste
- 1 tablespoon Asian fish sauce
- 5 pounds fresh mussels, scrubbed and debearded

1. Combine coconut milk, lime juice, white wine, curry paste, garlic, fish sauce, and sugar in a large pot.
2. Stir to dissolve sugar and curry paste; bring to a boil. Let mixture boil for 2 minutes, then add mussels.
3. Cover and cook, stirring occasionally, until mussels are opened, 5 to 8 minutes.
4. Remove the pot from heat and discard any unopened mussels.
5. Pour mussels and liquid into a serving dish and toss with cilantro.

Per Serving: Calorie: 485 / Carbs: 21g / Protein: 48g / Fat: 24g / Fiber: 1g

Chapter IV Poultry & Meat Recipes

HONEY GARLIC CHICKEN THIGHS

Serves 8 / Prep time: 10 minutes/ Cook time: 20 minutes

- 8 (5 ounces) boneless chicken thighs
- 2 tablespoons olive oil
- 7 cloves garlic, (or chopped)
- ½ cup soy sauce
- 1 pinch garlic powder, or to taste
- salt and ground black pepper
- ½ medium onion (chopped)
- 1 cup honey
- 1 pinch onion powder, or to taste
- ¼ cup chopped fresh cilantro

1. Season the chicken with salt and pepper on both sides
2. Brown the seasoned chicken in olive oil in a cast iron skillet for approximately 3-5 minutes on both sides.
3. Add onion and garlic, then cook for about 5-7 minutes till it's softened. Mix honey, soy sauce, onion powder and garlic powder in the skillet
5. Return the chicken to the skillet. Cook again for 10 minutes until the inner temperature is at least 165°F(74°C)
6. Place the cooked chicken on a plate. Drizzle the liquid from the pan over it and sprinkle cilantro. Then, serve.

Per Serving: Calories: 368 / Fat: 13g / Carbs: 38g / Fiber: 0g / Protein: 25g

BEEF AND BROCCOLI STIR-FRY

Serves 4 / Prep time: 10 minutes/ Cook time: 20 minutes

- 1 / 4 lbs flank steak thinly sliced
- 2 cups broccoli florets
- 1 / 4 cup oyster sauce
- 1 teaspoon sugar
- 1 teaspoon cornstarch salt and pepper to taste
- 1 tablespoon + 1 teaspoon vegetable oil divided use
- 2 teaspoons minced fresh ginger 1 teaspoon minced garlic
- 1 / 4 cup beef broth or water
- 2 teaspoons toasted sesame oil 1 teaspoon soy sauce

1. Heat 1 teaspoon oil in a pan and cook the broccoli for 4 minutes till it's tender Add ginger and garlic, then cook for 30 seconds. Remove broccoli; cover on a plate
2. Wipe the pan, heat 1 tablespoon of oil. Season and cook the steak in batches, 3-4 minutes per side. Return and cook broccoli for 2 minutes
3. Whisk oyster sauce, broth, sugar, sesame oil and soy sauce. Mix cornstarch with water. Pour sauce over beef and veggies; cook for 30 seconds; add cornstarch and boil briefly. Serve immediately (with rice if you desire)

Per Serving: Calories: 266 / Fat: 12g / Carbs: 6g / Fiber: 1g / Protein: 32g

TURKEY AND CRANNED BERRY STUFFED BELL PEPPERS

Serves 6 / Prep time: 15 minutes/ Cook time: 1 hour 10 minutes

- 6 medium / large bell peppers
- 2 medium shallots, chopped
- ¼ cups low sodium chicken or veggie broth
- 2 tsp brown sugar
- ½ cup raw pecans, chopped
- ¼ tsp pepper
- ¼ tsp dried thyme
- Fresh chopped parsley for garnish
- 1 tbsp olive oil
- 1 lb ground lean turkey
- 2 tsp apple cider vinegar
- ½ cup dried cranberries
- ½ tsp salt
- ¼ tsp dried rosemary
- ¾ cup shredded regular or dairy-free mozzarella cheese

1. Preheat the oven to 350°F.
2. Cut pepper tops, remove seeds, and place in a baking dish.
3. Sauté shallots, add turkey, broth, vinegar, and brown sugar. Cook until liquid evaporates.

4. Combine turkey mixture with rice, cranberries, pecans, salt, pepper, rosemary, and thyme.

5. Fill peppers, top with cheese, pour broth in the dish, cover with foil, and bake for 45- 50 minutes.

6. Remove foil, bake 5 more minutes, and garnish with fresh parsley.

Per Serving: Calories: 415 / Fat: 19g / Carbs: 33g / Fiber: 4g / Protein: 30g

BALSAMIC GLAZED CHICKEN DRUMSTICKS

Serves 3 / Prep time: 15 minutes/ Cook time: 30 minutes

- 6 chicken drumsticks
- 5 garlic cloves - minced
- 1 teaspoon soy sauce
- 75 ml balsamic vinegar
- 1 tsp freshly grated ginger
- 2 teaspoon water

1. Preheat oven to 200°C / 400°F

2. Mix the balsamic vinegar, garlic, ginger, and soy sauce ina bowl Arrange the drumsticks on a tray; brush with marinade

3. Bake for 35-40 minutes

4. Make the thick vinegar thin with 2 teaspoons of water.

5. Brush the meat with marinade; pour the remaining into the pan. Finish cooking in the oven.

6. Leave the drumsticks in the tray to enjoy the sticky residue. Serve with beer, crusty bread, and salads.

Per Serving: Calories: 272 / Fat: 14g / Carbs: 6g / Fiber: 1g / Protein: 27g

LAMB CHOPS WITH ROSEMARY AND GARLIC

Serves 2-3 / Prep time: 10 minutes/ Cook time: 10 minutes / marinate: 30 minutes

- 1 pound lamb rib chops
- 2 teaspoons salt
- 1 garlic clove, minced
- 2 tablespoons minced fresh rosemary
- 1 teaspoon freshly ground black pepper
- 4 tablespoons extra virgin olive oil, divided

1. Marinate the lamb chops with rosemary, salt, pepper, garlic, and 2 tbsp olive oil; let double rib chops stand at room temp for 30-45 mins.

2. For single rib chops, refrigerate if aiming for rare; marinate up to 24 hrs (allow double rib chops to stand 30-40 mins before cooking).

3. Sear chops in 2 tbsp olive oil over high heat, about 2-3 mins per side for double rib chops, 1 min per side for rare or medium-rare single rib chops.

4. Check doneness; if rare, they may be cooked enough; for more doneness, oven at 400°F for 3-5 mins or cover in the hot pan on low heat for a few mins.

5. Finger test for rib chops or aim for 125°F rare, 135°F medium-rare, 140°F medium with an instant-read thermometer for thick chops.

6. Rest cooked chops; remove from pan, cover with foil, and rest for 3-5 mins before serving.

Per Serving: Calories: 506 Fat: 37g / Carbs: 1g / Fiber: 0g / Protein: 43g

CHICKEN PICCATA

Serves 6 / Prep time: 10 minutes/ Cook time: 30 minutes

- 2 lbs butterfly-cut chicken breasts
- 1¾ tsp sea salt
- 10 tbsp unsalted butter + 4 tbsp olive oil
- 1 finely chopped shallot + 1 tbsp minced garlic
- 1½ cups chicken stock
- 2 tbsp drained capers
- ½ tsp cracked black pepper
- 1 cup flour
- 1 tsp lemon zest + 1 tbsp lemon juice

1. Season chicken with pepper and 1½ tsp salt; coat with flour.

2. Cook chicken in 3 tbsp butter and 2 tbsp oil, 2-3 mins per side.

3. Transfer to a serving platter. Cook shallot and garlic in the pan. Stir in stock; simmer for 4-5 mins.

4. Reduce heat; add 4 tbsp butter, capers, lemon zest, lemon juice, and ½ tsp salt.

5. Pour sauce over chicken. Garnish with parsley before serving.

Per Serving: Calories: 457 / Fat: 30g / Carbs: 19g / Fiber: 2g / Protein: 27g

PORK TENDERLOIN WITH APPLE CHUTNEY

Serves 6 / Prep time: 10 minutes/ Cook time: 1 hour

Roast Pork Loin:
- 1 boneless pork loin roast (2-2.5 lbs)
- 1 / 2 tsp black pepper
- 2 tsp kosher salt
- 1 tsp onion powder
- 1 / 2 tsp cayenne pepper

- 2 tbsp olive oil
- 2 tsp granulated garlic
- 2 tsp brown sugar
- 1 tsp smoked paprika

Apple Chutney:
- 1 tbsp olive oil
- 2 cups chopped apples
- 1-inch piece ginger
- 1 / 2 cup apple cider vinegar
- 1 clove garlic, minced

- 1 / 2 cup finely minced shallots
- 1 / 2 cup cranberries
- 1 / 4 tsp kosher salt
- 3 tbsp maple syrup
- 1 / 4 tsp cayenne pepper

Roast Pork Loin:
1. Pat dry, brush pork with olive oil.
2. Mix pepper, garlic, salt, brown sugar, onion powder, paprika, cayenne; rub on pork. Rest for 20 mins.
3. Preheat oven to 475°F. Roast pork for 15 mins, then lower to 350°F. Continue roasting for 45 mins or until internal temp is 145°F.
4. Rest for 10 mins before slicing.

Apple Chutney:
1. Heat olive oil, sauté shallots for 1 min. Add apples, cranberries, ginger, salt; cook for 2 mins.
2. Stir in vinegar, maple syrup, garlic, cayenne; simmer covered for 30 mins until thick. Adjust salt. Remove from heat and set aside to cool.

Per Serving: Calories: 628 / Fat: 22g / Carbs: 20g / Fiber: 2g / Protein: 83g

KOREAN BBQ BEEF BULGOGI

Serves: 4-6 / Prep time: 10 minutes/ Cook time: 10 minutes

MAIN:
- 800g thinly sliced ribeye or top sirloin
- 2 optional green onions, thinly sliced
- 1 tbsp toasted sesame oil
- 1 tbsp toasted sesame seeds

- 1 optional onion, thinly sliced
- 1 / 2 optional carrot, thinly sliced
- 1 tbsp cooking oil

BULGOGI MARINADE:
- 6 tbsp soy sauce
- 2 tbsp rice wine (mirin)
- 1 / 2 onion
- 1 tsp minced ginger

- 3 tbsp brown sugar
- 1 red apple or Asian pear
- 1 tbsp minced garlic
- 1 / 8 tsp ground black pepper

1. Blend marinade ingredients until smooth; set aside.
2. Mix thinly sliced meat with marinade, gently massaging. Add sesame oil separately.
3. Cover, marinate meat for at least 4 hours (or overnight for deeper flavor) in the fridge.
4. Preheat skillet / grill, add cooking oil, cook meat (and optional vegetables) for 3-5 mins on medium-high to high heat. Toss in sesame seeds, stir quickly.
5. Serve bulgogi with steamed rice and Korean side dishes.

Per Serving: Calories: 436 / Fat: 17g / Carbs: 18g / Fiber: 1g / Protein: 47g

CHICKEN AND SPINACH ENCHILADAS

Serves: 5 / Prep time: 20 minutes/ Cook time: 40 minutes

- 1 tbsp butter
- ½ cup sliced green onions 2 cloves minced garlic
- 2 large cooked chicken breasts, diced
- 10 oz frozen chopped spinach (thawed, drained, squeezed dry)

- ½ tsp chili powder
- ⅛ tsp salt
- ½ cup sour cream
- 1 ½ cups shredded Monterey Jack cheese (divided) 1 ½ cups shredded mozzarella cheese (divided)
- 5 (10-inch) flour tortillas
- ¼ tsp black pepper
- 1 cup ricotta cheese
- 2 (10 oz) cans enchilada sauce

1. Melt butter, cook green onions, and garlic until fragrant. Add chicken, spinach, chili powder, pepper, and salt; cook for 5 mins. Remove from heat.
2. Mix ricotta, sour cream, 1 cup Monterey Jack, and 1 cup mozzarella into chicken mixture. Reserve remaining cheeses for topping.
3. Warm tortillas in a bag in the microwave. Spoon 3 / 4 cup of chicken filling down the center of each tortilla, roll, and place seam sides down in a 9x13-inch baking dish.
4. Pour enchilada sauce over filled enchiladas, sprinkle the remaining 1 / 2 cup of cheese on top.
5. Bake at 375°F until filling bubbles and cheese is browned at the edges, about 30 mins.

Per Serving: Calories: 688 Fat: 35g / Carbs: 49g / Fiber: 5g / Protein: 43g

STEAK FAJITAS WITH PEPPERS AND ONIONS

Serves: 6 / Prep time: 15 minutes/ Cook time: 20 minutes
- 1 tbsp paprika
- 1 tsp ground cumin
- 1 / 2 tsp ancho chile powder
- Kosher salt
- Juice of 3 limes
- 4 bell peppers (red, orange, and / or yellow), thinly sliced
- 2 red onions, thinly sliced
- Toppings: shredded cheddar cheese, chopped fresh cilantro
- 2 tsp packed light brown sugar
- 1 1 / 2 tsp chili powder
- 1 / 2 tsp garlic powder
- 1 1 / 2 lbs skirt steak
- 3 tbsp extra-virgin olive oil
- 8 to 12 flour tortillas

1. Mix paprika, brown sugar, cumin, chili powder, ancho powder, garlic powder, and 1 tsp salt.
2. Marinate steak with lime juice, 1 tbsp olive oil, and spice mixture; refrigerate for 30 mins to 2 hours.
3. Sauté bell peppers and red onions in a skillet with 2 tbsp olive oil, lime juice, and 1 tsp salt, until charred and tender.
4. Preheat the grill, brush with olive oil. Grill steak 3-5 mins per side for medium rare; let rest 5-10 mins.
5. Warm the tortillas. Slice steak against the grain, season with salt. Serve on tortillas with onions, peppers; top with cheese and cilantro. Serve with lime wedges.

Per Serving: Calories: 589 / Fat: 28g / Carbs: 55g / Fiber: 6g / Protein: 31g

JAMAICAN JERK CHICKEN

Serves: 6 / Prep time: 10 minutes/ Cook time: 40 minutes
- 1 whole chicken (cut)

MARINADE
- 4-6 Scotch Bonnet peppers
- 4-6 garlic cloves
- 1 / 4 cup soy sauce
- 2 tbsp olive oil
- Juice of half a lime
- 2 tbsp brown sugar
- 1 tsp allspice
- 1 tsp dried thyme (or fresh if available) Salt and pepper to taste
- 1 small red onion
- 4 stalks scallions
- 1 / 4 cup vinegar (white or apple cider)
- About 3 / 4 cup orange juice
- 1 tbsp grated ginger
- 1 tsp nutmeg
- 1 tsp cinnamon

1. Make jerk marinade by blending all ingredients. Poke holes in chicken for deeper marination.
2. Place chicken in a bowl or sealable bag; cover completely with marinade.
3. Refrigerate for at least 2 hours or overnight. Discard marinade.
4. TO GRILL: Heat grill, oil grates, grill chicken for 12-20 mins until internal temp reaches 165°F.
5. TO BAKE: Preheat the oven to 400°F. Bake chicken for 35-40 mins until the internal temp is 165°F.
6. Grilling is traditional, but baking is easy. Remove from heat and serve.

Per Serving: Calories: 358 / Fat: 24g / Carbs: 9g / Fiber: 1g / Protein: 25g

GROUND TURKEY LETTUCE WRAPS

Serves: 8 / Prep time: 10 minutes/ Cook time: 10 minutes

- 1 tbsp sesame oil
- 1 / 4 cup shredded carrots
- 8 oz sliced water chestnuts, coarsely chopped
- 1 clove minced garlic
- 2 tbsp low sodium soy sauce
- 2 tsp red chili paste
- 1 lb ground turkey
- 6 oz mushrooms, coarsely chopped
- 2 green onions, chopped
- 1 / 4 cup hoisin sauce
- 1 tbsp rice wine vinegar
- 12 butter lettuce leaves

1. In a skillet, cook ground turkey in sesame oil until almost done.
2. Add carrots, mushrooms, water chestnuts, green onions, and garlic; cook 1-2 mins.
3. Combine hoisin sauce, soy sauce, rice wine vinegar, and chili paste. Stir into mixture; simmer for 1-2 mins. Then, serve.

Per Serving: Calories: 134 / Fat: 9g / Carbs: 11g / Fiber: 2g / Protein: 16g

ITALIAN SAUSAGE AND PEPPERS

Serves 6 / Prep time: 15 minutes/ Cook time: 45 minutes

- 6 (4 ounce) links sweet Italian sausage
- 1 medium yellow onion, sliced
- 4 cloves garlic, minced
- 1 medium green bell pepper, sliced
- 1 teaspoon dried oregano
- 2 tablespoons butter
- ½ medium red onion, sliced
- 1 large red bell pepper, sliced
- 1 teaspoon dried basil
- ¼ cup white wine, or more to taste

1. Brown sausage in skillet for 5-7 mins; remove and slice.
2. Melt butter; stir in onions and garlic for 2-3 mins.
3. Add bell peppers, season with basil and oregano, and stir in 1 / 4 cup wine. Cook until tender (5-7 mins).
4. Return sausage slices to the skillet.
5. Reduce heat to low, cover, and simmer for 15 mins.
6. Add more wine if needed. Serve hot and enjoy!

Per Serving: Calories: 461 / Fat: 39g / Carbs: 7g / Fiber: 2g / Protein: 17g

MAPLE DIJON GLAZED PORK CHOPS

Serves: 4 / Prep time: 12 minutes/ Cook time: 20 minutes

- 4 bone-in pork rib chops (1-inch thick)
- 2 tbsp chopped fresh tarragon leaves (or flat-leaf parsley for garnish)

Rub:
- 2 tsp sea salt
- 1 tsp marjoram
- 1 / 4 tsp garlic powder
- 2 tsp onion powder
- 1 / 2 tsp freshly ground black pepper
- 1 / 2 tsp herbes de Provence (optional)

Glaze:
- 1 / 2 cup real maple syrup
- 1 tbsp olive oil
- 1 / 4 cup Dijon mustard

1. Preheat the grill for high heat. In a small bowl, combine maple syrup, Dijon mustard, and olive oil; set aside.
2. Combine salt, onion and garlic powder, marjoram, pepper, and herbes de provence (if using). Pat onto both sides of pork chops.
3. Place chops on the grill and cook for 15 minutes, turning occasionally
4. During the last 3 to 4 minutes of cooking, brush on maple glaze. Cook for 1 minute, turn, and repeat. (Watch for flare-ups due to sugar content in maple syrup.)
5. Once chops are cooked, remove from heat, place on a platter, and let rest for 5 minutes.
6. Garnish with chopped tarragon or parsley leaves before serving.

Per Serving: Calories: 6275 / Fat: 383g / Carbs: 30g / Fiber: 1g / Protein: 632g

CHICKEN SHAWARMA WRAPS

Serves: 4 / Prep time: 25 minutes/ Cook time: 20 minutes / marinade time: 8 hours

Marinade:
- 2 lemons (juiced)
- ½ cup olive oil
- 6 minced garlic cloves
- 1 tsp kosher salt
- 2 tsp freshly ground black pepper
- 2 tsp ground cumin
- 2 tsp paprika
- ½ tsp turmeric
- A pinch of cinnamon
- ¼ - ½ tsp crushed red pepper flakes

Other Ingredients:
- 2 lbs boneless, skinless chicken breast cutlets
- 1 medium red onion (peeled, cut into eight wedges)
- ¾ cup plain fat-free Greek yogurt
- 2 tbsp light mayonnaise
- 1 tbsp lemon juice
- 1 tbsp stirred tahini
- ¼ tsp garlic powder
- 8 pitas
- 8 leaves green leaf lettuce
- 2 medium tomatoes (thinly sliced)
- ½ medium cucumber (thinly sliced)
- 2 tbsp chopped fresh parsley

1. Mix marinade: 2 lemons (juiced), ½ cup olive oil, 6 minced garlic cloves, 1 tsp kosher salt, 2 tsp black pepper, 2 tsp cumin, 2 tsp paprika, ½ tsp turmeric, pinch of cinnamon, ¼ - ½ tsp crushed red pepper flakes.
2. Marinate 2 lbs of chicken for 2-12 hours. Roast chicken and onions at 425°F for 16-22 mins.
3. Create white sauce: ¾ cup Greek yogurt, 2 tbsp light mayo, 1 tbsp lemon juice, 1 tbsp tahini, ¼ tsp garlic powder.
4. Assemble wraps: Pitas with lettuce, tomatoes, cucumbers, roasted onions, 2.875 oz sliced chicken, 2 tbsp white sauce, and parsley.

Per Serving: Calories: 298 / Fat: 12g / Carbs: 16g / Fiber: 1g / Protein: 35g

GRILLED LEMON HERB TURKEY BURGERS

Serves: 4 / Prep time: 15 minutes/ Cook time: 25 minutes

- 1 tbsp sunflower oil
- 1 onion, finely chopped
- 500g pack minced turkey
- Zest of 1 lemon
- 2 tsp fresh thyme leaves or 1 tsp dried
- 2 tbsp chopped parsley
- 4 thin rashers streaky bacon
- Buns, lettuce leaves, sliced tomato, and tomato sauce for serving.

1. Preheat oven to 200C / 180C fan / gas 6. Fry onion until browned; cool. Mix turkey with lemon zest, thyme, parsley, onion, and seasoning.
2. Shape into 4 burgers, wrap each in bacon, bake for 20-25 mins. Pan-fry briefly for crispy bacon. Serve in a bun with lettuce, tomato, sauce, and vegetable chips.

Per Serving: Calories: 206 / Fat: 8g / Carbs: 3g / Fiber: 1g / Protein: 31g

BEEF AND VEGETABLE KABOBS

Serves: 4 / Prep time: 25minutes/ Cook time: 8 hours 5 minutes

- ¾ cup balsamic vinegar
- ¾ cup extra-virgin olive oil
- 2 tablespoons whole-grain mustard
- 1 tablespoon dried oregano
- 1 tablespoon dried rosemary
- 2 cloves garlic, sliced
- ½ teaspoon salt
- ½ teaspoon ground pepper
- 1 pound tri-tip sirloin steak, trimmed and cut into 32 chunks
- 16 button mushrooms
- 16 cherry tomatoes
- 1 small bell pepper (any color), cut into 16 pieces
- 16 (1 inch) chunks red onion

1. Whisk together vinegar, oil, mustard, oregano, rosemary, garlic, salt, and pepper in a small bowl.
2. Skewer beef, mushrooms, tomatoes, bell pepper pieces, and onion chunks onto 8 metal or wooden skewers, alternating evenly.

3. Place kebabs in a 9-by-13-inch baking dish and pour the marinade over them. Refrigerate for at least 2 hours and up to 8 hours.
4. Preheat the grill to medium-high. Remove kebabs from the dish and discard marinade.
5. Grill the kebabs, turning once, to desired doneness, 6 to 8 minutes total. For campfire grilling, hold skewers over flames, turning regularly, until meat is cooked, about 15 minutes for medium.

Per Serving: Calories: 237 / Fat: 10g / Carbs: 12g / Fiber: 3g / Protein: 25g

CHICKEN PARMESAN

Serves: 4 / Prep time: 15 minutes/ Cook time: 20 minutes

- 4 skinless, boneless chicken breast halves
- 2 large eggs
- ¾ cup grated Parmesan cheese (divided)
- ½ cup olive oil for frying (or as needed)
- ¼ cup fresh mozzarella, cut into small cubes
- ½ cup grated provolone cheese
- Salt and freshly ground black pepper to taste
- 1 cup panko bread crumbs (or more as needed)
- 2 tablespoons all-purpose flour (or more if needed)
- ½ cup prepared tomato sauce
- ¼ cup chopped fresh basil
- 2 teaspoons olive oil

1. Preheat the oven to 450°F (230°C).
2. Pound chicken breasts to 1 / 2-inch thickness between plastic sheets. Season with salt and pepper; coat with flour.
3. Beat eggs in a bowl. Mix breadcrumbs and 1 / 2 cup Parmesan; set aside.
4. Dip chicken in eggs, then coat with breadcrumb mixture. Rest for 10-15 minutes.
5. Heat olive oil in a skillet, cook chicken until golden (2 minutes per side).
6. Transfer to a baking dish, top with tomato sauce, mozzarella, basil, provolone,
7. Parmesan, and drizzle with olive oil. Bake until cheese is browned, and chicken reaches 165°F (74°C), 15-20 minutes.

Per Serving: Calories: 471 / Fat: 25g / Carbs: 25g / Fiber: 1g / Protein: 42g

MOROCCAN LAMB TAGINE

Serves: 6-8 / Prep time: 30 minutes/ Cook time: 3 hours

- Olive oil
- 3 garlic cloves, crushed
- 1 tbsp ground cinnamon
- 1 tbsp sweet paprika
- 1.4kg British lamb shoulder, diced into 2cm cubes
- 250g stoned prunes, roughly chopped
- 1 tbsp sugar
- 400g tin chickpeas, drained and rinsed Juice ½ lemon
- 2 red onions, sliced
- 1 tbsp ground ginger
- 1 tbsp ground cumin
- 1 tbsp ground turmeric
- 2 x 400g tins chopped tomatoes
- 500ml chicken stock

1. Heat oil in a casserole, fry onions, add garlic and spices, cook for 2 minutes.
2. Season lamb, add to pot, cook for 5 minutes.
3. Add tomatoes, prunes, stock, and sugar. Simmer for 3 hours, adding water if needed.
4. In the last 30 minutes, stir in chickpeas and lemon juice.
5. Season with salt and pepper. Serve with parsley, coriander, pistachios, and pomegranate seeds.

Per Serving: Calories: 461 / Fat: 20.1g / Carbs: 22.2g / Fiber: 9g / Protein: 42.3g

PULLED CHICKEN SANDWICHES WITH COLESLAW

Serves: 1 / Prep time: 15 minutes/ Cook time: 1 hour

THE PULLED CHICKEN
- 1 teaspoon cooking oil
- 2-6 chipotle peppers in adobo sauce, finely minced
- ¼ cup Worcestershire sauce (gluten-free, if needed)

THE COLESLAW
- 2 cups finely shredded cabbage
- 1 medium carrot, grated

- 6 cloves garlic, minced
- 2 cups orange juice
- 1 tablespoon Dijon mustard

- ¼ cup chopped cilantro
- 1 tablespoon lime juice

- 2 teaspoons honey
- Pinch salt and pepper

PULLED CHICKEN SAUCE
1. Heat oil, garlic, and chipotle peppers in a pot. Add orange juice, Worcestershire sauce, dijon mustard, and sugar (if using).
2. Simmer chicken in the sauce for 1 hour until very tender. Shred the chicken, boil the sauce until thickened.

COLESLAW
1. Shred cabbage, add chopped cilantro and grated carrot. Mix lime juice, honey, salt, and pepper in a bowl. Combine coleslaw ingredients.

Per Serving: Calories: 544 / Fat: 22g / Carbs: 64g / Fiber: 3g / Protein: 24g

TERIYAKI BEEF SKEWERS

Serves 6 / Prep time: 40 minutes/ Cook time: 10 minutes

- 1 / 3 cup soy sauce
- 3 / 4 cup plus 2 tbsp water (divided) 6 tablespoons honey
- 1 tablespoon rice vinegar
- 1 tablespoon mirin rice wine 1 / 2 teaspoon sesame oil
- 1 teaspoon minced ginger
- 1 1 / 2 teaspoon minced garlic
- 1 tablespoon cornstarch
- 2 tablespoons cilantro leaves
- 2 pounds top sirloin steak (cut into 1 ½ inch cubes) 2 cups pineapple wedges (cut into 1 ½ inch cubes) 1 cup diced red onion (cut into 1 ½ inch cubes)
- ½ teaspoon sesame seeds
- 1 tablespoon sliced green onion

1. Whisk soy sauce, water, honey, rice vinegar, mirin, sesame oil, ginger, and garlic. Reserve ½ cup teriyaki sauce; marinate beef in the rest. Soak wooden skewers if using.
2. Boil the remaining sauce, add cornstarch slurry, set aside. Thread beef, pineapple, and red onion on skewers. Heat and grease grill.
3. Grill skewers, discarding marinade, 3 mins each side until internal temperature reaches 130°F (medium-rare) or 140°F (medium). Rest meat for 5 mins.
4. Glaze skewers with teriyaki sauce; garnish with sesame seeds, green onions, and cilantro.
5. Serve with extra teriyaki sauce.

Per Serving: Calories: 286 / Fat: 6g / Carbs: 22g / Fiber: 1g / Protein: 36g

BAKED ZESTY LIME CHICKEN THIGHS

Serves 6 / Prep time: 40 minutes/ Cook time: 10 minutes

- 4 bone-in, skin-on chicken thighs
- Salt and pepper, to taste
- 2 tablespoons olive oil
- ½ onion, diced
- 4 cloves garlic, minced
- 1 ½ cups chicken broth
- ½ cup chopped fresh cilantro (20 g), plus more for garnish
- 1 lime, juiced

1. Season chicken thighs with salt and pepper.
2. Heat olive oil in a skillet; cook chicken until golden brown. Remove chicken; sauté onion until translucent.
3. Add garlic, pour in chicken broth; place chicken on top. Remove chicken; stir in black beans, cilantro, and lime juice. Serve chicken over rice, garnished with cilantro. Enjoy!

Per Serving: Calories: 179 / Fat: 12g / Carbs: 7g / Fiber: 1g / Protein: 25g

Chapter V Beans & Legumes Recipes

LENTIL SOUP

Serves 4 / Prep time: 10 mins/ Cook time: 45 mins

- ¼ cup extra virgin olive oil
- 1 medium yellow or white onion, chopped
- 2 carrots, peeled and chopped
- 4 garlic cloves, pressed or minced
- 2 teaspoons ground cumin
- 1 teaspoon curry powder
- ½ teaspoon dried thyme
- 1 large can (28 ounces) diced tomatoes, lightly drained
- 1 cup brown or green lentils, picked over and rinsed
- 4 cups vegetable broth
- 2 cups water
- 1 teaspoon salt, more to taste
- Pinch of red pepper flakes
- Freshly ground black pepper, to taste
- 1 cup chopped fresh collard greens or kale, tough ribs removed
- 1 to 2 tablespoons lemon juice (½ to 1 medium lemon), to taste

1. Warm the olive oil in a large Dutch oven or pot over medium heat. Once the oil is shimmering, add the chopped onion and carrot and cook, stirring often, until the onion has softened and is turning translucent, about 5 minutes.
2. Add the garlic, cumin, curry powder and thyme. Cook until fragrant while stirring constantly, about 30 seconds.
3. Pour in the drained diced tomatoes and cook for a few more minutes, stirring often, in order to enhance their flavor.

Per Serving: Calorie: 366 kcal / Carbs: 47.8g / Protein: 14.5g / Fat: 15.5g / fiber: 10.8g

BLACK BEAN BURRITOS

Serves 2 / Prep time: 10 mins/ Cook time:15

- 2 (10 inch) flour tortillas
- 2 tablespoons vegetable oil
- 1 small onion, chopped
- ½ red bell pepper, chopped
- 1 teaspoon minced garlic
- 1 teaspoon minced jalapeno peppers
- 1 (15 ounce) can black beans, rinsed and drained
- 3 ounces cream cheese, cubed
- ½ teaspoon salt
- 2 tablespoons chopped fresh cilantro

1. Gather all ingredients. Preheat the oven to 350 degrees F (175 degrees C). Wrap tortillas in foil.
2. Bake wrapped tortillas in the preheated oven until heated through, about 15 minutes.
3. Heat oil in a 10-inch skillet over medium heat. Add onion, bell pepper, garlic, and jalapeño; cook and stir for 2 minutes.
4. Stir in beans and cook until heated through, about 3 minutes. Stir in cream cheese and salt; cook, stirring occasionally, for 2 minutes. Stir in cilantro.
5. Spoon filling in a line across the middle of each tortilla. Fold opposing edges of the tortilla to overlap the filling.
6. Roll 1 of the opposing edges around the filling creating a burrito. Serve immediately.

Per Serving: Calorie: 692 kcal / Carbs: 70g / Protein: 21g / Fat: 36g / Fiber: 15g

CHICKPEA SALAD WITH CUCUMBER AND FETA

Serves 4 / Prep time: 15 mins/ Cook time: 15 mins

- 2 tablespoons extra-virgin olive oil
- 2 tablespoons lemon juice
- ¼ teaspoon salt
- ¼ teaspoon ground pepper
- 1 15-ounce can of chickpeas, rinsed
- 2 cups diced cucumber
- ⅓ cup crumbled feta cheese
- ¼ cup finely chopped red onion
- ¼ cup diced red bell pepper
- 2 tablespoons chopped fresh dill

1. Stir oil, lemon juice, salt, and pepper together in a large bowl.
2. Add chickpeas, cucumber, feta, red onion, bell pepper, and dill; toss to coat.

Per Serving: Calorie: 183 kcal / Carbs: 15g / Protein: 6g / Fat: 11g / Fiber: 4g

RED BEANS AND RICE

Serves 8 / Prep time: 25 mins/ Cook time: 3 hrs 5 mins

- 1 pound dry kidney beans
- 1 large onion, chopped
- 2 stalks celery, chopped
- 6 cups water
- 1 tablespoon dried parsley
- 1 teaspoon Cajun seasoning
- ¼ teaspoon dried sage
- 4 cups water
- ¼ cup olive oil
- 1 green bell pepper, chopped
- 2 tablespoons minced garlic
- 2 bay leaves
- 1 teaspoon dried thyme
- ½ teaspoon cayenne pepper
- 1 pound andouille sausage, sliced
- 2 cups long-grain white rice

1. Rinse beans, and then soak in a large pot of water overnight.
2. Heat oil in a skillet over medium heat. Cook onion, bell pepper, celery, and garlic in olive oil for 3 to 4 minutes.
3. Rinse beans, and transfer to a large pot with 6 cups of water. Stir cooked vegetables into beans.
4. Season with bay leaves, parsley, thyme, Cajun seasoning, cayenne pepper, and sage. Bring to a boil, and then reduce heat to medium-low. Simmer for 2 1 / 2 hours.
5. Stir sausage into beans, and continue to simmer for 30 minutes.
6. Meanwhile, prepare the rice. Bring water and rice to a boil in a saucepan. Reduce heat, cover, and simmer for 20 minutes. Serve beans over steamed white rice.

Per Serving: Calorie: 630 kcal / Carbs: 79g / Protein: 24g / Fat: 24g / Fiber: 10g

THREE-BEAN CHILI

Serves 10 / Prep time: 10 mins/ Cook time: 4hrs

- 1 (20 ounces) package of 93%-lean ground turkey
- 1 (28-ounce) can of diced fire-roasted tomatoes • 1 (16 ounce) can tomato sauce
- 1 (15.5 ounces) can of pinto beans, rinsed and drained
- 1 (15.5 ounces) can of kidney beans, rinsed and drained
- 1 (15 ounces) can of reduced-sodium black beans, rinsed and drained
- 1 small onion, chopped
- 2 tablespoons chili powder
- 1 teaspoon oregano
- 1 (4.5 ounces) can of chopped green chiles
- 1 tablespoon minced garlic
- 1 pinch ground cumin

1. Cook and stir turkey in a large skillet over medium-high heat until crumbly and browned 7 to 10 minutes; transfer to a slow cooker.
2. Stir in tomatoes, tomato sauce, pinto beans, kidney beans, black beans, onion, green chilies, chili powder, garlic, oregano, and cumin in the slow cooker.
3. Cover and cook on Low for 7 hours or High for 4 hours.

Per Serving: Calorie: 238 kcal / Carbs: 29g / Protein: 20g / Fat: 5g / Fiber: 9g

HUMMUS AND VEGGIE WRAP

Serves 4 / Prep time: 5 mins

- 4 large flour tortilla wraps
- ½ large cucumber
- 1 avocado sliced into thin slices
- 1 small carrot julienned
- 4 teaspoons hot sauce or sriracha, optional
- 1 cup hummus
- 2 small Roma tomatoes sliced
- 1 yellow bell pepper sliced into thin slices
- 1 cup mixed salad greens

1. Warm up the tortilla wraps in the microwave or a skillet for 10 seconds. On each tortilla wrap, spread about 4 tablespoons of hummus.
2. Layer the sliced cucumber, tomato, avocado, bell pepper, and carrot. Top with mixed salad leaves. Drizzle with sriracha hot sauce.
3. Fold the sides of the tortilla inward over the fillings. You want to tuck these in so nothing falls out.
4. Then, fold the bottom of the tortilla up and over the fillings and the folded-in sides. Keep rolling the wrap away from you, making sure to tuck in the sides as you go.
5. Finish by pressing down a bit on the seam, where the tortilla edges meet, so it stays closed.

6. Slice in half, and serve with extra sauce on the side if desired.

Per Serving: Calorie: 294 kcal / Carbs: 33g / Protein: 9g / Fat: 2g / Fiber / 9g

WHITE BEAN AND KALE STEW

Serves 4 / Prep time: 5mins/ Cook time: 25 mins

- 2 tablespoons olive oil
- 1 small onion chopped
- 2 (15 ounces) cans of cannellini beans drained and rinsed (see note 1)
- 4 cups chicken broth (see note 2)
- 2 cups water
- 2 cups kale stems removed and torn into 1" pieces (see note 3)
- Salt and freshly ground black pepper

1. Heat the oil in a 3-quart saucepan over medium-high heat until it shimmers.
2. Add onion and cook until softened, about 5 minutes. Meanwhile, mash one can of beans in a small bowl.
3. Add mashed beans, broth, and water to the saucepan. Bring to a boil. Stir in the remaining beans and kale.
4. Reduce heat, partially cover, and simmer for about 20 minutes, until kale is tender.
5. Season to taste with salt and pepper (I like 1 teaspoon salt and ½ teaspoon pepper).

Per Serving: Calorie: 198 kcal / Carbs: 27g / Protein: 10g / Fat: 8g / Fiber: 7g

MEXICAN REFRIED BEANS

Serves 6 / Prep time: 10 mins/ Cook time: 10 mins

- 2 tablespoons canola oil
- 2 garlic cloves, peeled
- 2 (15-ounce) cans of pinto beans
- 1 teaspoon cumin
- 1 teaspoon chili powder
- salt to taste
- ½ lime, juiced

1. Heat canola oil in a heavy skillet over medium heat.
2. Cook garlic cloves in hot oil, turning once, until brown on both sides, 4 to 5 minutes.
3. Smash garlic cloves in the skillet with a fork.Heat canola oil in a heavy skillet over medium heat.
4. Cook garlic cloves in hot oil, turning once, until brown on both sides, 4 to 5 minutes. Smash garlic cloves in the skillet with a fork.

Per Serving: Calorie: 132 kcal / Carbs: 16g / Protein: 5g / Fat: 6g / Fiber: 5g

CURRIED CHICKPEAS WITH SPINACH

Serves 6 / Prep time: 5mins/ Cook time: 20 mins

- 3 tbsp sunflower or canola oil
- 1 large onion finely chopped
- 4 cloves garlic, crushed
- 1-inch ginger, finely grated
- 1 tbsp ground coriander
- 1 / 2 tbsp ground turmeric
- 1 / 2 tbsp ground cumin
- 1 / 4 - 1 / 2 tsp cayenne pepper or chili flakes
- 1.5 cups crushed tomatoes (400g)
- 2.5 cups cooked chickpeas (400g)
- 1 / 2 cup vegetable stock (120 ml)
- 1 cup frozen chopped spinach or 100 fresh / frozen chopped spinach
- 1 / 2 - 1 tsp salt
- 1 tsp sugar
- 1 tsp garam masala
- 1 tbsp lemon juice

1. Heat the oil in a large pan over a medium-high setting. Sauté the finely chopped onion until golden.
2. Add the crushed garlic and grated ginger and cook for 1-2 minutes, stirring frequently, until the garlic doesn't smell raw anymore.
3. Mix in ground coriander, turmeric, cumin, and cayenne and toast for two minutes stirring often.
4. Add the crushed tomatoes, chickpeas, and vegetable stock. Increase the heat to high and once boiling, lower to medium-low to maintain a simmer for 10 minutes, stirring now and then.
5. Add 1 / 2 tsp salt, the sugar, and the spinach. If the spinach is frozen, increase the heat until the curry is bubbling away again.
6. Simmer for an additional five minutes. Add the garam masala, lemon juice, and coconut milk and stir. Sprinkle over the chopped cilantro leaves and serve hot.

Per Serving: Calorie: 417 kcal / Carbs: 47g / Protein: 17g / Fat: 20g / Fiber: 10g

BLACK-EYED PEA SALAD

Serves 6 / Prep time: 15 mins

- 15-ounce can of black-eyed peas, drained and rinsed
- 6 ounces grape tomatoes, chopped
- ½ cup pomegranate arils, (arils of ½ pomegranate)
- 20 mint leaves, chopped
- 1 English cucumber, trimmed and chopped
- 2 green onions, chopped
- Feta cheese, optional

Dressing
- 2 tablespoon pomegranate molasses
- 4 tablespoons extra virgin olive oil
- Kosher salt & black pepper
- Juice of ½ lemon
- 1 garlic clove minced

1. In a large mixing bowl, combine the black-eyed peas, chopped tomatoes, cucumbers, pomegranate arils, onions, and fresh mint.
2. In a small bowl, whisk together the pomegranate molasses, lemon juice, olive oil, garlic, and a good dash of salt and pepper.
3. Pour the mixture over the black-eyed pea salad. Mix well to combine. Finish with a sprinkle of feta cheese, if you like.

Per Serving: Calorie: 190 kcal / Carbs: 25.6g / Protein: 6.5g / Fat: 7.7g / Fiber: 6.1g

LENTIL CURRY

Serves 5 / Prep time: 5 mins/ Cook time: 55 mins

- 50g (3 tbsp) butter, unsalted (tbsp neutral oil)
- 1.5 tbsp ginger, finely mince
- 2 tbsp curry powder, mild or spicy
- 1 / 2 tsp cayenne pepper, optional
- 1 / 2 tsp black pepper
- 4 garlic cloves, finely minced
- 1 onion, finely chopped (white, yellow, brown)
- 1 / 2 tsp turmeric powder
- 1 1 / 4 tsp salt
- 1 cup dried lentils, green or brown (or any other dried lentils or split peas,
- 400 ml / 14 oz coconut milk, full fat
- 3 cups (750 ml) water
- Yogurt, optional
- 400g / 14 oz canned tomato, crushed or diced
- 1 / 2 cup coriander / cilantro, finely chopped
- Basmati rice (or other rice)

1. Melt butter in a pot over medium heat. Add onion, garlic and ginger. Slowly cook, stirring now and then, for 10 minutes until tinged with gold and the onion is sweet.
2. Turn the heat up to high, add curry powder and turmeric, and stir for 1 1 / 2 minutes. Add remaining ingredients and stir.
3. Bring to a simmer, then place the lid on and adjust the heat to low / medium-low so it's simmering gently.
4. Simmer for 30 minutes, then remove the lid and simmer for a further 10 minutes to reduce the sauce. (Lentils should be soft, sauce should be thickened and creamy).
5. Stir through half the coriander, then taste and add more salt if needed.
6. Serve over basmati rice, sprinkled with more coriander and a dollop of yogurt.

Per Serving: Calories:414 kcal / Carbs:36g / Protein:14g / Fat:26g / Fiber: 15g

QUINOA AND BLACK BEAN STUFFED PEPPERS

Serves 6 / Prep time: 45 mins

- 6 medium red, orange, and / or yellow bell peppers
- 1 tablespoon extra-virgin olive oil
- 1 tablespoon minced garlic
- ¾ teaspoon chili powder
- 1 large yellow onion, chopped (about 2 cups)
- 1 teaspoon ground cumin
- 2 cups cooked tri-color quinoa
- 2 teaspoons minced chipotle chiles plus 1 Tbsp. adobo sauce from a can
- 1 (15 ounces) can of no-salt-added black beans, rinsed
- 1 (14.5 ounces) can no-salt-added diced tomatoes
- ¼ teaspoon salt
- 1 cup frozen corn
- 1 ½ cups shredded pepper Jack cheese

1. Preheat the oven to 375 degrees F. Cut off the stem end of each bell pepper. Chop the pepper tops to yield 1 cup.

2. Remove and discard seeds and membranes from peppers. Bring about 1 inch of water to a boil in a large saucepan fitted with a steamer basket.

3. Add the peppers; cover and steam until starting to soften, about 3 minutes. Remove the peppers and set aside.

4. Heat oil in a large skillet over medium heat. Add onion and the chopped pepper tops; cook, stirring occasionally, until the onion is translucent, about 5 minutes.

5. Stir in garlic, cumin, chili powder, chipotles, and adobo; cook, stirring constantly, until fragrant, about 1 minute.

6. Remove from heat and add quinoa, black beans, tomatoes, corn, and salt; fold until well combined.

7. Stand the peppers upright in an 11-by-7-inch baking dish. Spoon about 1 cup of quinoa mixture into each pepper, packing it in tightly. Cover the stuffed peppers with foil.

8. Bake the peppers until warmed through, about 10 minutes. Remove the foil and sprinkle the peppers evenly with cheese.

9. Bake, uncovered until the cheese melts and browns slightly, 5 to 8 minutes. Let rest for 5 minutes before serving.

Per Serving: Calorie: 350 kcal / l Carbs: 44g / Protein 16g / Fat: 13g / Fiber 10g

GREEK BUTTER BEAN SALAD

Serves 4 / Prep time:10 mins/ Cook time: 50 mins

- 1 / 2 tablespoon extra-virgin olive oil
- 2 medium cloves garlic, minced
- 1 / 4 cup canned tomato purée
- 1 teaspoon minced fresh dill
- 1 / 4 teaspoon dried oregano, preferably Greek
- Kosher salt and freshly ground black pepper
- 1 / 2 medium yellow onion, finely chopped
- 1 (14.5-ounce) can butter beans, drained and rinsed
- 1 1 / 2 teaspoons red wine vinegar
- 1 teaspoon minced flat-leaf parsley
- Pinch of ground cinnamon

1. Heat oil over medium heat in a medium skillet until it shimmers.
2. Add onion and garlic and cook, stirring, until tender and nearly translucent, about 6 minutes.
3. Add beans, tomato puree, vinegar, dill, parsley, oregano, and cinnamon.
4. Season with salt and pepper, bring to a simmer, and cook until flavors meld, about 3 minutes.
5. Refrigerate until ready to serve or cool to room temperature before serving.
6. This dish is best eaten at room temperature, so remove from the refrigerator 1 hour before serving

Per Serving: Calorie: 102 kcal / Carbs: 17g / Protein: 6g / Fat: 2g / Fiber: 5g

CUBAN BLACK BEAN SOUP

Serves 4 / Prep time: 10 mins/ Cook time: 2 hrs

- 1 tablespoon olive oil
- 1 red onion, peeled and roughly chopped (a tablespoon reserved for garnish)
- 1 green bell pepper, roughly chopped
- 2 teaspoons kosher salt, plus more to taste
- 2 teaspoons ground coriander
- 1 / 2 teaspoon crushed red pepper flakes
- 1 pound dried black beans, (that have been soaked in water for at least 4 hours)
- 4 1 / 2 cups water
- 1 / 4 cup sour cream
- 1 lime, quartered
- 6 garlic cloves, peeled
- 2 teaspoons ground cumin
- 1 teaspoon Mexican or Italian dried oregano
- 2 dried or fresh bay leaves
- 1 avocado, pitted and sliced
- Cilantro Leaves

1. Pour the black beans into a large bowl. Cover with filtered water fir 4 hours, Drain the beans and then proceed with the recipe.

2. In a medium to large pot, set over medium heat, add the olive oil. Add the onion, bell pepper, garlic, salt, ground cumin, coriander, oregano, and crushed red pepper.

3. Cook until softened and fragrant, about 5 minutes. Add the bay leaves, black beans, and water. Stir until combined.

4. Bring to a simmer and bring the heat down to medium-low. Cook for about 2 hours, until the beans are tender.

5. Remove the bay leaves and discard. Using an immersion blender, blend the black beans until they're smooth and cohesive. This will thicken the soup quite a bit.
6. Divide amongst bowls and garnish with avocado, a dollop of sour cream, some of the reserved red onion, and cilantro leaves.

Per Serving: Calories: 240kcal / Carbs: 20g / Protein: 10g / Fat: 5g / Fiber: 10g

SPICY CHICKPEA AND TOMATO STEW

Serves: 4 / Prep time: 10 mins/ Cook time: 25 mins

- 1 tbsp vegetable oil
- 2 garlic cloves, chopped
- 2 mild red chillies, thinly sliced
- ¾ tsp garam masala
- 4 tomatoes, chopped
- 400g can chickpea, rinsed and drained
- rice or naan bread, to serve
- 1 red onion, sliced
- ½ finger-length piece of fresh root ginger, shredded
- ½ tsp turmeric
- 1 tsp ground cumin
- 2 tsp tomato purée
- 200g baby spinach leaves

1. Heat the oil in a wok and fry the onion over low heat until softened.
2. Stir in the garlic, ginger, and chilies and cook for a few minutes and 5 minutes until the onions are golden and the garlic is slightly toasted.
3. Add the turmeric, garam masala, and cumin, stirring over low heat for a few seconds.
4. Tip in the chopped tomatoes and add the tomato purée, then simmer for 5 mins.
5. Add the chickpeas to the pan with 300ml water (fill the can three-quarters full). Simmer for 10 mins before stirring in the spinach to wilt

Per Serving: Calorie: 145 kcal / Carbs: 17g / Protein: 7g / Fat: 6g / Fiber: 5g

WHITE BEAN AND ROSEMARY DIP

Serves 16 / Prep time: 10 mins/ Cook time: 20 mins

- 2 tablespoons olive oil, plus extra for drizzling
- 2 teaspoons minced fresh rosemary
- 2 garlic cloves, peeled
- 1 (16 ounce) can white beans, undrained

1. Place olive oil, garlic, and rosemary in a 10-inch skillet. Heat the pan until the ingredients start to sizzle.
2. Add beans and their liquid to the pan. As beans cook, mash them with a wooden spoon or potato masher.
3. Cook until mixture is a loose spread consistency (it will thicken as it cools). Transfer to a serving bowl or storage container.

Per Serving: Calorie: 48 kcal / carbs: 6g / Protein: 2g / Fat:2g / Fiber: 1g

VEGETARIAN LENTIL SLOPPY JOES

Serves 8 / Prep time: 15 mins/ Cook time: 39 mins

- 1 tablespoon olive oil
- 1 small onion finely diced
- 1 cups water
- 1 cup brown lentils
- ¼ cup ketchup
- 1 teaspoon Worcestershire sauce
- 1 teaspoon chili powder
- 1 tablespoon cider vinegar
- 1 green bell pepper finely chopped
- 3 cloves garlic minced
- 1 cup broth beef or vegetable broth
- 1 cup tomato sauce
- 3 tablespoons tomato paste
- 2 tablespoons brown sugar
- 1 teaspoon yellow mustard
- 8 hamburger buns

1. Cook green pepper and onion in olive oil until softened, about 4 minutes. Add garlic, water, broth and lentils.
2. Bring to a boil and reduce heat to simmer. Cover and cook for 25 minutes.
3. Stir in remaining ingredients (except buns) and simmer for an additional 10-15 minutes or until thickened.
4. Spoon lentil mixture over hamburger buns and serve

Per Serving: Calories: 266 / Carbs: 47g / Protein: 12g / Fat: 4g / Fiber: 10g

CHICKPEA AND VEGETABLE STIR-FRY

Serves 2 / Prep time: 5 mins/ Cook time: 15 mins

- 1 Tablespoon oil
- 3 cloves garlic, minced
- 400 g tin chickpeas, drained (240g, or ~ 1 ¼ cups, when drained)
- 3 Tablespoons dark soy sauce
- 450 g mixed stir-fry vegetables 300 g fresh noodles
- ½ Tablespoon sesame seeds
- 1 mild red chili, finely chopped (see notes below)
- 1 Tablespoon honey (or agave)
- A few sprigs of fresh coriander (cilantro), chopped

1. Heat the oil in a wok or large, deep frying pan. Add the finely chopped chili and garlic, along with the drained chickpeas.
2. Cook over medium-high heat for a few minutes, until fragrant.
3. Add all of the vegetables and stir-fry for another 5 minutes, stirring regularly, until the vegetables are just tender.
4. Move the vegetables to the side of the pan to create a space in the center.
5. Add the soy sauce and honey to the space, and allow the sauce to begin bubbling and sizzling.
6. Cook for a minute or so, then add the noodles and mix everything.
7. Cook over medium-high heat for a few more minutes, until the noodles are hot and the vegetables are cooked to your liking.

Per Serving: Calories: 510 kcal - Carbs: 80.3 g - Protein: 20.5 g - Fat: 13.4g / Fiber: 11.7g

BLACK BEAN AND CORN SALAD

Serves 6 / Prep time: 25 mins

- ½ cup olive oil
- 1 clove garlic, minced
- ⅛ teaspoon ground cayenne pepper
- 1 ½ cups frozen corn kernels
- 1 red bell pepper, chopped
- 6 green onions, thinly sliced
- ⅓ cup fresh lime juice
- 1 teaspoon salt
- 2 (15-ounce) cans of black beans, rinsed and drained
- 1 avocado - peeled, pitted and diced
- 2 tomatoes, chopped
- ½ cup chopped fresh cilantro

1. Place olive oil, lime juice, garlic, salt, and cayenne pepper in a small jar.
2. Close the lid tightly and shake the jar until the dressing is well combined.
3. Combine in a salad bowl beans, corn, avocado, bell pepper, tomatoes, green onions, and cilantro.
4. Shake dressing again, pour over salad, and toss to coat.

Per Serving: Calories 391 kcal / Carbs: 35g / Protein: 11g / Fat: 25g / Fiber: 12g

TUSCAN WHITE BEAN BRUSCHETTA

Serves 45 / Prep time: 5 mins/ Cook time: 10 mins

- 1 / 2 loaf sliced Ciabatta (or other Italian) bread
- 1 can (15 ounces) cannellini (white) beans, drained and rinsed
- 2 teaspoons fresh lemon juice
- Kosher or sea salt, to taste
- 1 / 2 cup coarsely chopped walnuts, toasted
- Chopped flat-leaf parsley or fresh basil, for garnish
- 1 / 4 cup extra virgin olive oil, divided
- 1 teaspoon chopped garlic
- Fresh ground black pepper, to taste
- 2 tablespoons white truffle oil (or more to taste)

1. Preheat the broiler or grill. Brush bread slices with olive oil, using around 3 tablespoons.
2. Place the oiled side down on the grill or on a cookie sheet around 4 inches from the broiler.
3. Cook for 4 to 5 minutes or until toasted and light golden brown.
4. Remove from the oven; turn pieces from the grill over so the oiled side is up. Set on a large cookie sheet.
5. In a food processor, mix the beans, lemon juice, garlic, and remaining 1 tablespoon olive oil and purée until creamy and smooth.
6. Season to taste with salt and pepper. Spread purée on toast pieces and sprinkle walnuts on the top.
7. Drizzle with truffle oil and garnish with chopped parsley. Move from a baking sheet to a pretty platter and serve.

Per Serving: Calorie: 180 kcal / Carbs: 22g / Protein: 6g / Fat: 7g / Fiber: 3g

ROASTED BRUSSELS SPROUTS WITH BALSAMIC GLAZE

Serves 6 / Prep time: 30 mins

- 1½ pounds Brussels sprouts, halved, stems and ragged outer leaves removed*
- 3 tablespoons extra virgin olive oil
- ¾ teaspoon kosher salt
- ½ teaspoon freshly ground black pepper
- 1 tablespoon balsamic vinegar
- 1 teaspoon honey

1. Preheat the oven to 425°F and set an oven rack in the middle position. Line a baking sheet with heavy-duty aluminum foil.
2. Directly toss the Brussels sprouts on the prepared baking sheet with 2 tablespoons of the oil, the salt, and the pepper.
3. Roast, stirring once halfway through, until tender and golden brown, about 20 minutes.
4. Drizzle the remaining tablespoon of oil, the balsamic vinegar, and the honey over the roasted Brussels sprouts.
5. Toss to coat evenly. Taste and adjust seasoning, if necessary, then serve.

Per Serving: Calorie: 116 kcal / Carbs: 12g / Protein: 4g / Fat: 7g / fiber: 4g

STEAMED ASPARAGUS WITH LEMON BUTTER

Serves 4 / Prep time: 5 mins/ Cook time: 10 mins

- 1 bunch fresh asparagus medium thickness (about 20 spears)
- 2 tablespoons butter melted
- 1 teaspoon lemon juice freshly squeezed
- ½ teaspoon Diamond Crystal kosher salt or ¼ teaspoon of fine salt
- ¼ teaspoon black pepper freshly ground
- ¼ teaspoon garlic powder

1. Pour 1 inch of water into a saucepan. Fit a steamer basket into the saucepan. Bring the water to a boil.
2. Chop off about an inch from the bottom of the asparagus. Once the water has boiled, place the asparagus in the steamer basket.
3. Cover and steam until the asparagus is just barely tender, about 5 minutes. Thinner spears will require just 3 minutes of steaming.
4. Immediately remove the asparagus from the steamer and transfer it to a serving platter.
5. Drizzle it with melted butter and lemon juice, and sprinkle it with kosher salt, black pepper, and garlic powder. Serve immediately.

Per Serving: Calories: 70kcal / Carbs: 4g / Protein: 2g / Fat: 6g / Fiber: 2g

GRILLED ZUCCHINI AND YELLOW SQUASH

Serves 6 / Prep time: 20 mins

- 2 tablespoons extra-virgin olive oil
- 2 cloves garlic, minced
- 2 large zucchini, sliced lengthwise into 1 / 2-inch-thick slices
- 2 large summer squash, sliced lengthwise into 1 / 2-inch-thick slices
- 1 teaspoon ground pepper
- ¾ teaspoon salt
- 1 ½ tablespoons finely chopped fresh parsley
- 1 ½ tablespoons lemon juice

1. Preheat grill to medium-high (400-450°F). Combine olive oil and garlic in a small bowl.
2. Brush zucchini and squash with the oil mixture; sprinkle with pepper and salt.
3. Oil the grill grates by partially soaking a few paper towels in canola oil and using tongs to quickly wipe the grates.
4. Place the vegetables on the oiled grates; grill, covered, until the zucchini and squash are just tender and grill marks appear, 2 to 3 minutes per side.
5. Transfer the vegetables to a serving platter. Sprinkle with parsley and drizzle with lemon juice.

Per Serving: Calorie: 82 kcal / Carbs: 7g / Protein: 3g / Fat: 5g / Fiber:2g

QUINOA AND ROASTED VEGETABLE SALAD

Serves 1 / Prep time: 5mins

- 2 cups mixed salad greens
- ½ cup cooked quinoa
- 1 tablespoon crumbled feta cheese
- 1 cup roasted root vegetables
- 1-2 tablespoons vinaigrette
- 1 tablespoon sunflower seeds

1. Combine greens, roasted vegetables, and quinoa; drizzle with vinaigrette. Top the salad with feta and sunflower seeds.
2. Assemble the recipe, cover it, and store it in the refrigerator for up to 1 day.
3. If storing for more than 1 day, refrigerate mixed greens separately and combine with the other ingredients just before serving.

Per Serving: Calorie: 351 kcal / Carbs: 39g / Protein: 10g / Fat: 18g / Fiber: 9g

SAUTEED SPINACH WITH GARLIC

Serves 4 / Prep time: 5 mins/ Cook time: 5 mins

- 1 tablespoon unsalted butter
- 2 (10-ounce) bags of fresh spinach
- ½ teaspoon garlic salt, or to taste
- 6 cloves garlic, thinly sliced
- ½ medium lemon, juiced

1. Melt butter in a pot over medium heat. Add garlic; cook and stir until fragrant, about 2 minutes.
2. Add spinach, a few handfuls at a time, stirring until wilted before adding more.
3. Stir in lemon juice and season with garlic salt.

Per Serving: Calorie: 68 kcal / Carbs: 8g / Protein: 4g / Fat: 4g / Fiber: 4g

CAULIFLOWER MASH

Serves 4 / Prep time: 15 mins/ Cook time: 10 mins

- 1 head cauliflower, cut into florets
- 1 clove garlic, smashed
- 1 tablespoon reduced-fat cream cheese
- ⅛ teaspoon freshly ground black pepper
- 1 tablespoon olive oil
- ¼ cup grated Parmesan cheese
- ½ teaspoon kosher salt

1. Place a steamer insert into a saucepan; fill with water just below the bottom of the steamer.
2. Bring water to a boil; add cauliflower, cover, and steam until tender, about 10 minutes.
3. Meanwhile, heat olive oil in a small skillet over medium heat; cook and stir garlic until softened about 2 minutes. Remove from heat.
4. Transfer 1 / 2 of the cauliflower to a food processor; cover and blend on high. Add remaining cauliflower florets, one at a time, until vegetables are creamy.
5. Blend in cooked garlic, Parmesan cheese, cream cheese, salt, and black pepper.

Per Serving: Calorie: 98 kcal / Carbs: 8g / Protein: 5g / Fat: 6g / Fiber: 4g

BROCCOLI AND CHEDDAR STUFFED SWEET POTATOES

Serves 4 / Prep time: 15 mins/ Cook time: 1hr 10 mins

- 2 sweet potatoes, skin on
- 1 / 2 head broccoli, cut into florets
- 4 slices bacon, cut into small bits
- Salt and pepper, to taste
- 1 tbsp coconut sugar
- 2 tbsp butter or olive oil for dairy-free
- 1 cup mushrooms, sliced
- 1 tbsp olive oil
- 1 / 4 cup balsamic vinegar

1. Rinse the potatoes well. Line a baking tray with parchment paper and bake the potatoes at 400° for 35-50 minutes until tender.
2. Remove from the oven and let cool a little bit. Meanwhile, heat 1 tbsp olive oil in a large pan, and add the broccoli. Saute for 5 minutes, stirring frequently.
3. Remove the pan content, and add the bacon bits. Cook until crispy and slightly brown. Add the

mushroom slices and cook for 3 minutes more.

4. While the potatoes are still warm cut them into halves, lengthwise. Use a fork to fluff the flesh, and add the butter. Stir until it melts.
5. Top with mushroom-broccoli saute and bacon bits.
6. While the veggies are cooking, place the balsamic vinegar together with the coconut sugar in a small pot.
7. Simmer for 10 minutes until it thickens a bit. Drizzle over the potatoes before serving.

Per Serving: Calories: 259 kcal / CarbsS: 19g / Protein: 4g / Fat: 18g / Fiber: 2g

CUCUMBER AND TOMATO SALAD WITH BASIL

Serves 12 / Prep time: 15 mins/ Cook time: 8hrs

- 2 cups fresh baby spinach
- 2 tablespoons fresh basil
- 1 pound Campari tomatoes, seeded and minced
- 2 large seedless cucumbers, peeled and minced
- 1 large red onion, minced
- 3 cloves garlic, minced
- 1 teaspoon salt, or to taste
- 1 teaspoon cracked black pepper, or to taste

1. Process spinach and basil in a food processor until finely chopped.
2. Toss together spinach mixture, tomatoes, cucumbers, red onion, garlic, salt, and pepper in a large bowl with an airtight lid.
3. Cover the bowl and refrigerate salad, for 8 hours overnight.

Per Serving: 20 kcal / Carbs: 4g / Protein: 1g / Fat: 0 / Fiber: 1g

ROASTED SWEET POTATO WEDGES

Serves 6 / Prep time:15 mins/ Cook time: 23 mins

- 3 medium sweet potatoes
- 2 tablespoons extra virgin olive oil
- 1 teaspoon kosher salt plus additional for serving
- 1 teaspoon garlic powder
- 1 / 4 teaspoon chipotle chile powder use less if sensitive to spice or omit
- ¼ teaspoon ground black pepper
- ¼ teaspoon dried rosemary

1. Place a rack in the center of your oven and preheat the oven to 450 degrees F. Scrub and dry the sweet potatoes. Peel them if you like.
2. Cut each sweet potato in half lengthwise. Cut each half into 3 or 4 long spears about ¾-inch. Place the spears on a rimmed baking sheet and drizzle with the oil.
3. In a small bowl, stir together the salt, garlic powder, chipotle chile powder, black pepper, and rosemary.
4. Sprinkle over the potatoes and toss to coat, ensuring the wedges are evenly coated with the oil and spices.
5. Arrange the sweet potato wedges into a single layer, being careful that the wedges do not touch.
6. Bake the sweet potato wedges for 15 minutes, then turn over with a spatula. Return the pan to the oven and bake for another 5 to 10 minutes, until lightly browned and tender when pierced with a fork.
7. Turn the oven to broil. Broil the sweet potatoes for 3 to 5 minutes, until they are crisped at the edges to your liking. Remove from the oven and immediately sprinkle with a pinch of additional salt. Enjoy!

Per Serving: Calorie: 141 kcal / Carbs: 23g / Protein: 2g / Fat: 5g / Fiber: 3g

SAUTEED KALE WITH CRANBERRIES AND ALMONDS

Serve 4 / Prep time: 5 mins/ Cook time: 10 mins

- 1 bunch of kale (roughly 5-6 cups), stems removed and leaves chopped
- ¼ cup dried cranberries
- ¼ cup sliced almonds
- 2 tablespoons balsamic vinegar
- Salt and pepper to taste

1. Prepare the Kale: Start by washing and drying the kale leaves thoroughly. Toast the Almonds.
2. Preheat a large skillet or pan over medium-high heat and add the chopped kale. As the kale starts to wilt pour in the balsamic vinegar.
3. Stir the kale to evenly distribute the vinegar. Continue to cook for about 3-5 minutes, or until the kale is tender but still vibrant green. Season with black pepper to taste.
4. Once the kale is cooked to your desired tenderness, remove it from the heat and place it in a large bowl.

5. Toss in the toasted almonds and dried cranberries. These add delightful sweetness and crunch to the dish. Now, give everything a gentle stir to combine.

Per Serving: Calorie: 99 kcal / Carbs: 13.3g / Protein: 2.8g / Fat: 4.8g / Fiber: 2.4g

GRILLED EGGPLANT WITH TOMATO AND FETA

Serves 4 / Prep time: 45 mins/ Cook time: 20 mins

- 1 large eggplant
- 3 large heirloom tomatoes - to closely match the diameter of the eggplant
- 1 tbsp olive oil
- 4 garlic cloves - minced
- Juice from half a lemon
- ½ cup fresh basil leaves
- ¼ cup reduced-fat feta cheese crumbles
- Salt and pepper to taste

1. Cut the eggplant crosswise into ½" thick rounds. Lightly season them with salt and leave them for 30 minutes on a side to let water come out of the eggplant.
2. Lightly mist each slice with an olive oil mister and grill them on a grill rack that's been lightly sprayed with non-stick cooking spray for about 2-3 minutes on each side.
3. Finely chop the basil leaves, and combine them with olive oil, lemon juice, garlic, and salt & pepper.
4. Cut the tomatoes into 1 / 4" thick rounds. Spray a small baking sheet with non-stick cooking spray and preheat oven to 400 degrees.
5. Arrange 4 eggplant rounds side by side. Spread about 1 / 2 tablespoon of the basil-garlic mixture on top of each one, then sprinkle feta crumbs.
6. Top each with tomato rings. Add another layer of eggplant, basil spread, feta, and tomato rounds, and top with the rest of the crumbled feta.
7. Bake for 15 minutes. Serve immediately.

Per Serving: Calories: 119 kcal Carbs: 14g / Protein: 4g / Fat: 5g / Fiber: 6g

MASHED CAULIFLOWER WITH GARLIC AND HERBS

Serves 4 / Prep time:15 mins/ Cook time: 10 mins

- 1 head cauliflower, cut into florets
- 1 clove garlic, smashed
- 1 tablespoon reduced-fat cream cheese
- ⅛ teaspoon freshly ground black pepper
- 1 tablespoon olive oil
- ¼ cup grated Parmesan cheese
- ½ teaspoon kosher salt

1. Place a steamer insert into a saucepan; fill with water just below the bottom of the steamer.
2. Bring water to a boil; add cauliflower, cover, and steam until tender, about 10 minutes.
3. Meanwhile, heat olive oil in a small skillet over medium heat; cook and stir garlic until softened about 2 minutes. Remove from heat.
4. Transfer 1 / 2 of the cauliflower to a food processor; cover and blend on high. Add remaining cauliflower florets, one at a time, until vegetables are creamy.
5. Blend in cooked garlic, Parmesan cheese, cream cheese, salt, and black pepper.

Per Serving: Calorie: 98 kcal / Carbs: 8g / Protein: 5g / Fat: 6g / Fiber: 4g

SPAGHETTI SQUASH PRIMAVERA

Serves 6 / Prep time: 15 mins/ Cook time: 30 mins

- 1 spaghetti squash
- 1 onion, chopped
- 1 large zucchini, cut into bite-size pieces
- 1 tablespoon dried Italian herb seasoning
- 1 ½ cups chopped tomato
- 2 tablespoons extra-virgin olive oil
- 1 large clove garlic, minced
- 1 green bell pepper, chopped
- fresh ground black pepper, to taste
- ¾ cup crumbled feta cheese

1. Pierce the shell of spaghetti squash with a fork and place in a microwave-safe dish; cook in the microwave on high for 12 minutes. Set aside until cool enough to handle.
2. Slice squash in half lengthwise; remove seeds. Use a fork to pull the flesh away from the shell and place into a large bowl; fluff with the fork to separate strands as much as possible.
3. Heat olive oil in a large skillet over medium heat. Cook and stir onion in hot oil until just tender, about 3

minutes.

4. Add garlic; cook and stir for another 3 minutes. Stir zucchini and green bell pepper into mixture; season with Italian herb seasoning and black pepper.
5. Pour tomatoes into the skillet. Continue cooking just until tomatoes are warmed, 3 to 5 minutes.
6. Add squash strands to the skillet and toss until evenly mixed. Sprinkle with feta cheese and toss again to serve.

Per Serving: Calorie: 158 kcal / Carbs: 16g / Protein: 5g / Fat: 10g / Fiber: 2g

GREEN BEAN ALMONDINE

Serves 4 / Prep time: 10 mins/ Cook time: 15mins

- 1 pound fresh green beans
- 2 tablespoons butter
- salt and ground black pepper to taste
- 1 ½ ounces slivered almonds
- 2 cloves garlic, minced, or more to taste

1. Place beans into a microwave-safe casserole dish with enough water to cover the bottom. Microwave on high power until almost tender, 8 to 10 minutes.
2. Drain in a colander and refresh under cold running water to keep the nice green color.
3. Heat a frying pan over medium heat. Add almonds and cook until just starting to turn golden, about 3 to 5 minutes, watching closely to not burn.
4. Take the pan off of heat and add butter to melt. Return to heat and add garlic.
5. Mix in green beans, season with salt and pepper, and continue to stir until heated through 3 to 5 minutes. / Prep time: Calorie: 152 kcal / Carbs: 11g / Protein: 4g / Fat: 12g / Fiber: 4g

STUFFED BELL PEPPERS WITH QUINOA AND BLACK BEANS

Serves 6 / Prep time: 25 mins / Cool time: 20 mins

- 6 medium red, orange, and / or yellow bell peppers
- 1 tablespoon extra-virgin olive oil
- 1 tablespoon minced garlic
- ¾ teaspoon chili powder
- 2 teaspoons minced chipotle chiles plus 1 Tbsp. adobo sauce from a can
- 2 cups cooked tri-color quinoa
- 1 (14.5 ounces) can no-salt-added diced tomatoes
- ¼ teaspoon salt
- 1 large yellow onion, chopped (about 2 cups)
- 1 teaspoon ground cumin
- 1 (15 ounces) can of no-salt-added black beans, rinsed
- 1 cup frozen corn
- 1 ½ cups shredded pepper Jack cheese

1. Preheat oven to 375 degrees F. Cut off the stem end of each bell pepper. Chop the pepper tops to yield 1 cup.
2. Remove and discard seeds and membranes from peppers. Bring about 1 inch of water to a boil in a large saucepan fitted with a steamer basket.
3. Add the peppers; cover and steam until starting to soften, about 3 minutes. Remove the peppers and set aside.
4. Heat oil in a large skillet over medium heat. Add onion and the chopped pepper tops; cook, stirring occasionally, until the onion is translucent, about 5 minutes.
5. Stir in garlic, cumin, chili powder, chipotles, and adobo; cook, stirring constantly, until fragrant, about 1 minute.
6. Remove from heat and add quinoa, black beans, tomatoes, corn, and salt; fold until well combined.
7. Stand the peppers upright in an 11-by-7-inch baking dish. Spoon about 1 cup of quinoa mixture into each pepper, packing it in tightly. Cover the stuffed peppers with foil.
8. Bake the peppers until warmed through, about 10 minutes. Remove the foil and sprinkle the peppers evenly with cheese.
9. Bake, uncovered until the cheese melts and browns slightly, 5 to 8 minutes. Let rest for 5 minutes before serving.

Per Serving: Calorie: 350 kcal / Carbs: 44g / Protein: 16g / Fat: 13g / Fiber: 10g

ROASTED GARLIC PARMESAN ASPARAGUS

Serve 6 / Prep time: 10 mins/ Cook time: 10 mins

- 3 tablespoons extra-virgin olive oil
- ½ teaspoon ground pepper
- 1 ½ pounds fresh asparagus, trimmed
- 3 tablespoons whole-wheat panko breadcrumbs
- 2 cloves garlic, minced
- ¼ teaspoon salt
- ½ cup finely grated Parmesan cheese
- 3 tablespoons chopped walnuts

1. Preheat oven to 425 degrees F. Line a large-rimmed baking sheet with foil or parchment paper.
2. Combine oil, garlic, pepper, and salt in a large bowl; add asparagus and massage to evenly coat.
3. Spread the asparagus in an even layer on the prepared baking sheet.
4. Toss Parmesan, panko, and walnuts together in a small bowl; sprinkle over the asparagus.
5. Roast until the panko is golden and the asparagus is tender, 12 to 15 minutes. Serve immediately.

Per Serving: Calorie: 149 kcal / Carbs: 8g / Protein: 5g / Fat: 12g / Fiber: 3g

MEDITERRANEAN QUINOA SALAD

Serves 6 / Prep time: 15 mins/ Cook time: 20 mins

- ½ cup extra-virgin olive oil
- 3 tablespoons chopped fresh oregano
- 1 ½ teaspoons Dijon mustard
- 3 cups cooked quinoa, cooled (see Associated Recipes)
- 2 cups thinly sliced English cucumber
- 1 cup halved grape tomatoes
- 1 (15 ounces) can no-salt-added chickpeas, rinsed
- 1 cup crumbled feta, divided
- 6 tablespoons red wine vinegar
- 1 ½ teaspoons honey
- ¼ teaspoon crushed red pepper
- 1 ½ cups thinly sliced red onion
- ½ cup halved pitted Kalamata olives
- 3 cups baby spinach (about 3 ounces)

1. Whisk oil, vinegar, oregano, honey, Dijon, and crushed red pepper in a large bowl.
2. Add quinoa, cucumber, onion, tomatoes, olives, chickpeas, and 1 / 2 cup feta.
3. Toss gently to combine. Cover and refrigerate for 30 minutes.
4. Add spinach, and gently toss to combine. Sprinkle with the remaining 1 / 2 cup feta and serve immediately

Per Serving: 472 kcal / Carbs: 39g / Protein: 12g / Fat: 7g / Fiber: 7g

BAKED SWEET POTATO FRIES

Serves 4 / Prep time: 10/ Cook time: 20 mins

- 2 large sweet potatoes
- ½ teaspoon sea salt
- ¼ teaspoon garlic powder
- 3 tablespoons soybean oil (often labeled "vegetable oil")
- ½ teaspoon freshly ground black pepper
- ¼ teaspoon paprika

1. Gather all ingredients. Preheat the oven to 425 degrees F (220 degrees C).
2. Position the rack in the upper third of the oven. Grease a baking sheet.
3. Peel sweet potatoes and cut into 1x3-inch wedges.
4. Place wedges and soybean oil in a large bowl; toss lightly. Sprinkle with salt, pepper, garlic powder, and paprika.
5. Arrange potatoes in a single layer on the prepared baking sheet, being sure not to overcrowd.
6. Bake, turning occasionally, until tender and golden brown, 18 to 24 minutes. Cool for 5 minutes before serving.

Per Serving: Calorie: 120 kcal / Carbs: 10g / Protein: 1g / Fat: 10g / Fiber: 2g

STIR-FRIED BOK CHOY WITH GINGER

Serves 4 / Prep time: 3 mins/ Cook time: 3mins

- 6 small bok choys, up to ~17cm / 7" long, or other Asian greens (Note 1 + photos in post)
- 2 tbsp vegetable oil
- 1 / 4 cup water
- 1 1 / 2 tsp light soy sauce, or all-purpose soy (Note 2)
- 1 tsp oyster sauce (sub vegetarian oyster sauce)
- 2 tsp Chinese cooking wine (Note 3)
- 1 / 4 cup water
- 1 / 4 cup ginger, finely julienned (or 1 tbsp garlic)
- 3 tsp cornflour / cornstarch
- 1 tsp sesame oil, toasted
- 1 / 4 tsp cooking salt

1. Trim the base of the bok choy then separate all the leaves. Leave the delicate baby bok choy in the center intact, it's precious!
2. Cut giant stems in half lengthwise so they are all roughly the same size. Rinse in a colander, and shake off excess water.
3. Stir Sauce ingredients except water in a jug until cornflour is dissolved. Then stir in water.
4. Put the ginger and oil in a large non-stick pan. Turn on medium heat. Once the ginger starts sizzling, sauté for 1 minute until it turns light golden and is a bit floppy.
5. Add bok choy then use 2 spatulas to toss the ginger for around 15 seconds to coat.
6. Turn the heat up to medium, and pour water over. Cover with a lid and steam for just 45 seconds.
7. Remove lid (bok choy will still be a bit underdone), pour in the sauce, and toss for 30 seconds until the sauce changes from murky to clear, and thickens.
8. Bok choy should be just floppy but still soft crunch, not mushy. If your sauce gets too thick add a tiny splash of water and mix.
9. Pour the bok choy and all the sauce onto a serving plate, then eat!

Per Serving: Calories:81 kcal / Carbs:4g / Protein:2g / Fat:7g / Fiber: 1g

CAPRESE SALAD WITH AVOCADO

Serve 6 / Prep time: 5 mins/ Cook time: 5 mins

- 3 tablespoons balsamic vinegar
- ½ teaspoon salt
- 1 ½ cups multicolored cherry tomatoes, halved
- 4 ounces small fresh mozzarella balls
- ½ cup lightly packed fresh basil leaves
- 2 tablespoons extra-virgin olive oil
- ½ teaspoon ground pepper
- 2 ripe avocados, diced
- 1 tablespoon drained capers (optional)

1. Whisk vinegar, oil, salt, and pepper together in a small bowl.
2. Combine tomatoes, avocados, mozzarella, and capers (if using) in a large bowl.
3. Add the dressing and basil; toss to coat.

Per Serving: Calorie: 218 kcal / Carbs: 9g / Protein: 5g / Fat: 19g / Fiber: 5g

ROASTED ACORN SQUASH WITH MAPLE GLAZE

Serves 4 / Prep time: 10 mins/ Cook Time: 50 mins

- 2 Acorn Squash, mine were 1 1 / 2 lbs each
- 4 Tbsp unsalted butter, divided
- 1 / 2 tsp fine sea salt, plus more to taste
- 2 tsp extra light olive oil
- 2 Tbsp pure maple syrup, plus more for serving
- 1 / 2 tsp ground cinnamon

1. Preheat the oven to 400°F. Line a rimmed baking sheet with parchment paper for easier cleanup.
2. Carefully cut the squash in half from the tip through the stem. Start by inserting the knife deep into the side of the squash then cut through to the tip.
3. Once you have cut through the tip, stand the squash up on the stem side and cut through the stem.
4. Scrape out the strings and seeds with a spoon. Place squash on a baking sheet cut-side-up.
5. Brush the cut sides of the acorn squash with olive oil.
6. Add 1 Tablespoon of butter into each acorn squash half and drizzle each half with 1 / 2 Tbsp maple syrup. Sprinkle with salt and cinnamon.
7. Bake for 45-60 minutes, depending on squash size, or until squash is tender when pierced with a knife.
8. To infuse flavor, serve, transfer squash to a platter, cut the squash in half if desired, drizzle with more maple syrup, and sprinkle with salt to taste.

Per Serving: Calories: 232kcal / Carbs: 775mg / Protein: 2g / Fat: 14g: Fiber:3g

LEMON HERB ROASTED VEGETABLES

Serves 4 / Prep time: 10 mins/ Cook time: 35mins

- 1 red onion roughly chopped
- 1 aubergine cut into half-moons
- 125 grams kalamata olives pitted
- 250 grams cherry tomatoes
- 1 courgette sliced
- 1 red pepper roughly chopped
- 1 head of garlic broken into cloves and peeled
- 1 lemon cut into wedges

- 4 tbsp olive oil
- salt and pepper

1. Preheat your oven to 200 C / 400 F / gas mark 6
2. Arrange the chopped vegetables, lemon, and garlic on a sheet pan.
3. Drizzle over the olive oil and salt and pepper, and toss the vegetables carefully to ensure they are all coated.
4. Roast in the center of the oven for 30-45 minutes or until the vegetables are soft.

Per Serving: Calories:255.76kcal / Carbs:21.2g / Protein: 3.97g / Fat: 19.45g / Fiber: 7.39g

GREEK TZATZIKI CUCUMBER SALAD

Serves 1 / Prep time: 10 mins

- 1 cup plain Greek yogurt 240 g
- 1 Tbsp lemon juice 15 mL
- ¼ tsp each salt and pepper
- ¼ cup sliced red onion ¼ of a medium onion
- 1 Tbsp chopped fresh dill
- 1 clove garlic minced
- 1 cucumber thinly sliced

1. In a medium bowl, combine yogurt, dill, lemon, garlic, salt, and pepper.
2. Pat dry cucumber slices with paper towels.
3. Gently stir to combine yogurt dressing with cucumber and red onion.

Per Serving: Calories: 49 kcal / Carbs: 5.3g / Protein: 2g / Fat: 2.4g / Fiber: 0.4g

GRILLED PORTOBELLO MUSHROOMS WITH BALSAMIC GLAZE

Serves 3 / Prep time:10 mins/ Cook Time:10 mins

- 3 large portobello mushrooms
- ¼ cup balsamic vinegar
- 4 cloves garlic, minced
- ¼ cup canola oil
- 3 tablespoons chopped onion

1. Clean mushrooms; remove stems, reserving them for another use. Place mushroom caps gill-side up in a shallow dish.
2. Combine oil, balsamic vinegar, onion, and garlic in a small bowl.
3. Pour mixture evenly over mushroom caps; let marinate at room temperature for 1 hour.
4. Preheat the grill to medium-high heat; grease the grate.
5. Grill over the hot grill until caramelized and tender, about 5 minutes per side; serve warm.
6. close up view of Portobello Mushrooms with chopped mushrooms on top of a grill

Per Serving: Calories: 217 / Carbs: 11g / Protein: 3g / Fat 19g / Fiber 2g

ROASTED CARROTS WITH HONEY AND THYME

Serves 8 / Prep time: 5 mins/ Cook time: 30 mins

- 1kg Chantenay carrots, unpeeled, larger ones halved
- few thyme sprigs
- 25g butter
- 1 tbsp honey

1. Tip the carrots into a deep frying pan with the butter, thyme and honey. Cook for 5 mins until starting to brown.
2. Pour in 250ml water, bring to a boil, and cook until the water has evaporated and the carrots are tender.
3. Turn down the heat and cook the carrots slowly, stirring, until glazed.

Per Serving: Calorie: 73 kcal / Carbs: 11g / Protein: 1g / Fat: 3g / Fiber / 3g

Chapter VII Family Favorites Recipes

CLASSIC SPAGHETTI BOLOGNESE

Serves 6 / Prep time: 15 mins/ Cook time: 1hr 30 mins

- 1 tbsp olive oil
- 2 medium onions, finely chopped
- 2 celery sticks, finely chopped
- 2-3 sprigs of rosemary leaves picked and finely chopped
- 4 rashers smoked streaky bacon, finely chopped
- 2 carrots, trimmed and finely chopped
- 2 garlic cloves finely chopped
- 500g beef mince

For the bolognese sauce
- 2 x 400g tins plum tomatoes
- small pack of basil leaves picked, ¾ finely chopped and the rest left whole for garnish
- 1 tsp dried oregano
- 2 tbsp tomato purée
- 1 red chili deseeded and finely chopped
- 6 cherry tomatoes sliced in half
- 75g parmesan grated, plus extra to serve
- crusty bread to serve
- 2 fresh bay leaves
- 1 beef stock cube
- 125ml red wine
- To season and serve
- 400g spaghetti

1. Put a large saucepan on medium heat and add 1 tbsp olive oil. Add 4 finely chopped bacon rashers and fry for 10 mins until golden and crisp.
2. Reduce the heat and add the 2 onions, 2 carrots, 2 celery sticks, 2 garlic cloves, and the leaves from 2-3 sprigs of rosemary, all finely chopped, then fry for 10 mins. Stir the veg often until it softens.
3. Increase the heat to medium-high, add 500g beef mince, and cook stirring for 3-4 mins until the meat is browned all over.
4. Add 2 tins plum tomatoes, the finely chopped leaves from ¾ small pack basil, 1 tsp dried oregano, 2 bay leaves, 2 tbsp tomato purée, 1 beef stock cube, 1 deseeded and finely chopped red chili, 125ml red wine and 6 halved cherry tomatoes.
5. Stir with a wooden spoon, breaking up the plum tomatoes. Bring to the boil, reduce to a gentle simmer, and cover with a lid. Cook for 1 hr 15 mins stirring occasionally, until you have a rich, thick sauce.
6. Add the 75g grated parmesan, check the seasoning and stir. When the bolognese is nearly finished, cook 400g of spaghetti following the pack instructions.
7. Drain the spaghetti and either stir into the bolognese sauce or serve the sauce on top. Serve with more grated parmesan, the remaining basil leaves, and crusty bread, if you like.

Per Serving: Calorie: 624 kcal / Carbs: 58g / Protein: 35g / Fat: 25g / Fiber: 6g

CHICKEN ALFREDO PASTA

Serves 3 / Prep time: 2mins/ Cook time: 13 mins

- 200 g / 7oz chicken breast, cut in half horizontally
- 1 tbsp olive oil
- 2 cups milk, any fat %
- 1 large garlic clove, minced
- 3 / 4 cup freshly grated parmesan (Note 2)
- Salt and pepper
- 250 g / 8 oz fettuccine
- 1 1 / 2 cups chicken stock / broth
- 1 / 2 cup thickened / heavy cream (Note 1)
- Parsley, for garnish

1. Sprinkle both sides of the chicken with salt and pepper. Use a skillet large enough to fit the pasta.
2. Heat oil over medium-high heat. Add chicken and cook for 2 minutes on each side until golden and cooked through.
3. Remove onto a plate and rest for 5 minutes, then slice while the pasta is cooking. Add milk, chicken broth, and garlic. Bring to a simmer then add pasta.
4. Move pasta around every 30 seconds or so until it is softened (around 3 minutes) so it doesn't stick. Once pasta is softened, reduce heat to medium and stir every couple of minutes.
5. At about 9 - 10 minutes, the pasta should be almost cooked but there should still be liquid covering the

base of the skillet.

6. Add cream and parmesan and mix. Simmer, stirring occasionally, for ~2 minutes, until sauce is thickened and pasta is cooked.

7. Adjust salt and pepper to taste and serve immediately, garnished with freshly grated parmesan and parsley!

Per Serving: Calorie: 491 kcal / Carbs: 34g / Protein: 33.3g / Fat: 24.4g / Fiber: 1.1g

BEEF TACOS WITH ALL THE FIXINGS

Serves 5 / Prep time: 15 mins/ Cook time:20 mins

- 1 tbsp avocado oil (or other neutral oil of choice)
- 1 / 2 cup chopped onion (red, yellow, or white onion all work)
- 1 tbsp minced garlic
- 2 tbsp taco seasoning
- 1 tbsp tomato paste
- salt
- guacamole
- shredded iceberg lettuce
- Mexican shredded cheese
- 1 lb ground sirloin (90 / 10, which means 90% lean / 10% fat)
- 1 / 2 tsp cornstarch whisked with 1 / 4 cup of water
- taco shells for serving
- black pepper
- tomato salsa
- sour cream

1. In a large skillet, heat the oil over medium heat, and add the onion. Season with 1 / 8 tsp salt, and cook for 5 minutes until slightly softened.

2. Add the garlic and cook for 30 seconds, until fragrant. Turn the heat up to medium-high and add the ground beef.

3. Season with 1 / 2 tsp salt and 1 / 4 tsp black pepper, and brown the beef for 3-4 minutes, stirring frequently.

4. Add the taco seasoning, and keep cooking for 2-3 minutes, until no pink remains in the beef.

5. Add the cornstarch water slurry and the tomato paste, and cook for 3 more minutes, until the cornstarch thickens the liquid in the pan.

6. Taste the beef, and make any necessary adjustments with salt and pepper before removing the skillet from the heat.

7. Serve the ground beef in taco shells with the toppings of your choice. Enjoy!

Per Serving: calories: 252 kcal, carbs: 2g, Protein: 21g, fat: 17g Fiber: 1g

BAKED MACARONI AND CHEESE

Serves 6 / Prep time: 10 mins/ Cook time: 35 mins

- 1 (12 ounce) package of macaroni
- 1 egg
- 2 tablespoons butter, melted
- 2 cups milk
- 2 ½ cups shredded Cheddar cheese
- salt and pepper to taste

1. Preheat the oven to 350 degrees F (175 degrees C). Lightly grease a 2-quart baking dish.

2. Boil macaroni in a large pot of salted water until barely done, about 5 minutes. Drain and set aside.

3. Whisk together milk and egg in a large bowl. Stir in cheese and butter.

4. Place par-boiled macaroni in the prepared baking dish. Pour milk mixture over macaroni, season with salt and pepper, and stir until combined.

5. Press the mixture evenly into the baking dish. Bake, uncovered, in the preheated oven until the top is browned, 30 to 40 minutes. Serve hot and enjoy!

Per Serving: Calorie:472 kcal / Carbs: 46g / Protein: 22g / Fat:22g / Fiber:2g

HOMEMADE MARGHERITA PIZZA

Serves: 4 / Prep time: 25 mins/ Cook time: 10 mins

- 300g strong bread flour
- 1 tsp salt
- For the tomato sauce
- handful fresh basil or 1 tsp dried
- 1 tsp instant yeast (from a sachet or a tub)
- 1 tbsp olive oil, plus extra for drizzling
- 100ml passata
- 1 garlic clove, crushed

- For the topping
- handful grated or shaved parmesan
- To finish

- 125g ball mozzarella, sliced
- handful of cherry tomatoes, halved
- handful of basil leaves (optional)

1. Put the flour into a large bowl, then stir in the yeast and salt. Make a well, pour in 200ml warm water and the olive oil, and bring together with a wooden spoon until you have a soft, fairly wet dough.
2. Turn onto a lightly floured surface and knead for 5 mins until smooth. Cover with a tea towel and set aside.
3. Mix the passata, basil, and crushed garlic, then season to taste. Leave to stand at room temperature while you get on with shaping the base.
4. If you've let the dough rise, give it a quick knead, then split it into two balls. On a floured surface, roll out the dough into large rounds, about 25 cm across, using a rolling pin.
5. Heat the oven to 240C / 220C fan / gas 8. Put another baking sheet or an upturned baking tray in the oven on the top shelf.
6. Smooth sauce over the bases with the back of a spoon. Scatter with cheese and tomatoes, drizzle with olive oil, and season. Put one pizza, still on its baking sheet, on top of the preheated sheet or tray.
7. Bake for 8-10 mins until crisp. Serve with a little more olive oil, and basil leaves if using. Repeat the step for the remaining pizza.

Per Serving: Calorie:431 kcal / carbs:59 g / protein: 19g / fat: 15g / fiber 3g

GRILLED CHEESE SANDWICHES WITH TOMATO SOUP

Serves 8 / Prep time: 20 mins/ Cook time: 1hr

- 1 1/2 kg Tomatoes
- 2 tbsp olive oil
- 1 tsp salt
- 2 garlic cloves finely chopped
- 2 tsp tomato paste
- ½ cup cream
- fresh basil to serve
- 2 slices of bread per person
- 2 cups grated mature cheddar

- 2 tbsp balsamic vinegar
- 1 tbsp sugar
- 2 red onions finely chopped
- ½ cup fresh basil
- 8 cups vegetable / chicken stock
- salt & black pepper to taste
- for the grilled cheese sandwich
- 2 cups grated mozzarella
- Butter

1. Preheat the oven to 200°C / 390°F.
2. Place the tomatoes (if using canned tomatoes, add all the juices as well) in a roasting tray and add the Balsamic vinegar, olive oil, sugar, and salt.
3. Stir to combine and place in the oven for 25-30 minutes until the tomatoes are broken down and have started to caramelize.
4. In a large pot, sauté the onions in some olive oil until they are translucent and fragrant. Add the garlic and basil and fry for another minute.
5. Add the roasted tomatoes, tomato paste, and sugar. Stir to combine all the ingredients and pour in the stock.
6. Lower the heat and cover the pot. Allow to simmer for 10 minutes. Remove the pot from the heat and blend the soup.
7. Add the cream and season to taste. To make the grilled cheese sandwiches, mix the mozzarella with the cheddar.
8. Add ½ cup cheese to half of the slices of bread. Sandwich with the remaining bread. Butter both sides generously.
9. Cook in a non-stick pan, over medium heat until the cheese is melted and the sandwiches are golden brown on both sides.
10. Serve the tomato soup with a swirl of cream and fresh basil leaves with the grilled cheese sandwiches.

Per Serving: Calories: 479 kcal / Carbs: 41g / Protein: 22g / Fat: 26g / Fiber: 5g

BBQ PULLED PORK SLIDERS

Serves: 12 / Prep time: 10 mins/ Cook time: 7mins

- 12 Hawaiian slider rolls
- 1 pound pulled pork
- 6 slices White cheddar cheese

Glaze
- 3 tablespoons butter melted
- 1 teaspoon Italian seasoning

- 2 tablespoons butter
- 2 / 3 cup barbecue sauce
- 1 / 2 pound bacon chopped in 2 – 3" pieces

- 2 tablespoons brown sugar
- 1 teaspoon minced garlic

1. Preheat the oven to 350°F. Place sliders on a baking sheet and cut in half.
2. Spread 1 tablespoon of butter on both the top and bottom of the slider rolls. Place in the oven for a few minutes until the bread is slightly browned.
3. Warm pulled pork with barbecue sauce. Spread warmed pulled pork with barbecue sauce evenly across slider rolls.
4. Add slices of cheese evenly on top of the pork. Sprinkle bacon evenly on the cheese.
5. Place the top layer of the sliders on the sandwiches. Glaze and Melt butter and stir in the remaining glaze ingredients.
6. Spoon over slider rolls and bake for 5 – 10 minutes until cheese is melted and buns begin to brown on top.

Per Serving: Calories: 344 kcal / Carbohydrates: 24g / Protein: 14g / Fat: 22g / Fiber: 1g

CHICKEN PARMESAN

Serves 4 / Prep time: 15 mins / Cook time: 20 mins
- 4 skinless, boneless chicken breast halves
- 2 large eggs
- ¾ cup grated Parmesan cheese, divided
- ½ cup olive oil for frying, or as needed
- ¼ cup fresh mozzarella, cut into small cubes
- ¼ cup chopped fresh basil
- 2 teaspoons olive oil

- salt and freshly ground black pepper to taste
- 1 cup panko bread crumbs, or more as needed
- 2 tablespoons all-purpose flour, or more if needed
- ½ cup prepared tomato sauce

- ½ cup grated provolone cheese

1. Preheat the oven to 450 degrees F (230 degrees C). Whisk water and egg together in a bowl until smooth.
2. Combine bread crumbs, 2 tablespoons of Parmesan cheese, oregano, basil, thyme, and garlic powder in a separate bowl.
3. Dip each chicken breast in the egg mixture, allowing the excess egg to drip back into the bowl. Coat each chicken breast in bread crumb mixture, shaking off excess.
4. Repeat dipping each coated chicken breast in egg mixture and the bread crumb mixture for a double-coating and place in the prepared baking dish.
5. Spray breaded chicken breasts with cooking spray. Bake in the preheated oven for 40 minutes.
6. Pour spaghetti sauce over each chicken breast and top each with mozzarella cheese and remaining Parmesan cheese.
7. Continue baking until chicken is no longer pink in the center and the cheeses are melted, about 15 minutes more.
8. An instant-read thermometer inserted into the center should read at least 165 degrees F (74 degrees C).

Per Serving: Calories 395 kcal / Carbs33g / Protein 37g / Fat 12g / Fiber 4g

VEGETABLE STIR-FRY WITH TOFU OR CHICKEN

Serves 6 / Prep time: 20/ Cook time: 1hr5mins
- 2 tablespoons olive oil
- 1 tablespoon reduced-sodium soy sauce
- 1 teaspoon dry mustard
- 8 ounces cooked chicken breast, cubed
- 8 ounces tub-style extra-firm tofu (fresh bean curd), drained and cubed
- 2 medium carrots, bias-sliced, or 2 stalks celery, thinly sliced
- 1 cup sliced fresh mushrooms and / or fresh or frozen, thawed pea pods
- 3 cups hot cooked brown rice or rice

- 2 tablespoons orange juice
- 1 tablespoon Worcestershire sauce
- 1 teaspoon ground turmeric

- 2 cups chopped baby bok choy and / or fresh bean sprouts
- 3 green onions, cut into 1 / 2-inch-long pieces
- 1 medium red or green sweet pepper, cut into thin bite-size strips
1. In a large bowl, stir together 1 tablespoon of the oil, the orange juice, soy sauce, Worcestershire sauce, ginger, mustard, and turmeric.
2. Add cooked chicken and tofu cubes; stir to coat. Cover with plastic wrap or foil and marinate in the refrigerator for 1 to 4 hours.
3. In a very large nonstick skillet, heat the remaining 1 tablespoon of oil over medium-high heat.
4. Add carrot or celery; cook and stir for 2 minutes. Add mushrooms and / or pea pods; cook and stir for 2 minutes.
5. Add bok choy and / or bean sprouts, green onions, and sweet pepper; cook and stir for 2 minutes.
6. Add undrained chicken mixture; heat through. Serve with hot cooked rice.

Per Serving: Calorie: 285 / kcal / Carbs: 30g / Protein: 20g / Fat: 9g / Fiber:4g

BEEF AND VEGETABLE STIR-FRY

Serves 4 / Prep time: 25 mins/ Cook time:10mins

- 2 tablespoons vegetable oil
- 1 ½ cups fresh broccoli florets
- 2 carrots, thinly sliced
- 1 teaspoon minced garlic
- 2 tablespoons sesame seeds, toasted
- 1 pound beef sirloin, cut into 2-inch strips
- 1 red bell pepper, cut into matchsticks
- 1 green onion, chopped
- 2 tablespoons soy sauce

1. Heat vegetable oil in a large wok or skillet over medium-high heat; cook and stir beef until browned 3 to 4 minutes.
2. Move beef to the side of the wok and add broccoli, bell pepper, carrots, green onion, and garlic to the center of the wok.
3. Cook and stir vegetables for 2 minutes. Stir beef into vegetables and season with soy sauce and sesame seeds.
4. Continue to cook and stir until vegetables are tender, about 2 more minutes. Serve hot and enjoy!

Per Serving: Calories 268kcal / Carbs 9g / Protein 23g / Fat: 16g / Fiber: 3g

CHICKEN ENCHILADAS

Serves 8 / Prep time: 15 mins/ Cook time: 25 mins

- 1 tablespoon olive oil, or as needed
- 1 onion, chopped
- ½ pint sour cream
- ½ teaspoon dried oregano
- 1 (15 ounce) can tomato sauce
- 1 clove garlic, minced
- ½ teaspoon salt (Optional)
- 8 (10 inch) flour tortillas
- 4 skinless, boneless chicken breast halves
- 1 ¾ cups shredded Cheddar cheese, divided
- 1 tablespoon dried parsley
- ½ teaspoon ground black pepper
- ⅓ cup chopped green bell pepper
- 1 tablespoon chili powder
- ½ cup water (Optional)
- 1 (12 ounce) jar taco sauce

1. Preheat the oven to 350 degrees F (175 degrees C). Heat oil in a nonstick skillet over medium heat.
2. Add chicken and cook until no longer pink and juices run clear, 5 to 7 minutes per side.
3. Transfer chicken to a cutting board and slice into cubes. Return chicken to the skillet.
4. Add onion, 1 cup Cheddar cheese, sour cream, parsley, oregano, and black pepper. Cook and stir over low heat until the cheese melts.
5. Stir in tomato sauce, green pepper, garlic, chili powder, and salt. Add water if needed.
6. Spoon chicken mixture into tortillas and roll into enchiladas. Arrange enchiladas, seam-side down, in a 9x13-inch baking dish. Top with taco sauce and remaining 3/4 cup Cheddar cheese.
7. Bake in the preheated oven, uncovered, until the cheese has melted, about 20 minutes. Let cool briefly before serving.

Per Serving: Calorie: 498kcal / Carbs:50g / Protein:27g / Fat: 16g / Fiber: 4g

CREAMY CHICKEN AND RICE CASSEROLE

Serve 6 / Prep time: 10 mins/ Cook time: 1hr

- 3 chicken breasts, cut into cubes
- 2 cups instant white rice
- 1 (10.75 ounces) can of cream of celery soup
- salt and ground black pepper to taste
- 2 cups water
- 1 (10.75 ounces) can of cream of chicken soup
- 1 (10.75 ounces) can of cream of mushroom soup
- ½ cup butter, sliced into pats

1. Gather all ingredients.Preheat the oven to 400 degrees F (200 degrees C). Grease the sides and bottom of a casserole dish.
2. Stir chicken, water, rice, cream of chicken soup, cream of celery soup, and cream of mushroom soup together in the prepared casserole dish; season with salt and pepper.
3. Overhead of chicken rice casserole ingredients resting in a baking dish unmixed. Arrange butter evenly over the top of the chicken mixture.
4. Overhead of chicken rice casserole mixture resting in a baking dish with cuts of butter on top.
5. Bake in a preheated oven until the rice is tender and the chicken is cooked through, 1 hour to 75 minutes. Cool for 10 to 15 minutes before serving.

Per Serving: Calorie: 441kcal / Carbs: 37g / Protein: 17g / Fat: 25g / Fiber: 1g

TURKEY MEATBALL SUBS

Serves 8 / Prep time: 35 mins/ Cook time: 22 mins

- 2 large eggs
- ½ cup finely chopped parsley
- 4 cloves garlic, minced
- 1 24-oz. jar marinara sauce
- 2 ½ tablespoons extra-virgin olive oil
- ⅓ cup seasoned bread crumbs
- ⅔ cup finely grated Parmesan
- 2 pounds lean ground turkey
- 8 crusty sub-style rolls
- 12 ounces sliced provolone

1. Whisk eggs with 3 Tbsp. water. Stir in bread crumbs; let stand for 5 minutes.
2. Add Parmesan, parsley, garlic, and turkey; mix gently until well combined. Moisten hands and roll mixture into 24 1 1 / 2-inch balls.
3. Transfer to a dish large enough to accommodate all meatballs. Refrigerate meatballs for 30 minutes.
4. Pour marinara into a wide, deep pot with a lid and warm over medium-high heat.
5. Add meatballs (sauce will not completely cover meatballs), cover, and cook for 10 minutes. Uncover and turn meatballs.
6. Cover; cook 10 minutes longer, until meatballs are no longer pink inside
7. Preheat the broiler to high. Cut rolls lengthwise and drizzle inside of each with 1 tsp. olive oil.
8. Divide cheese among rolls and place on baking sheet. Broil until cheese is melted and bread is lightly toasted 1 to 2 minutes.
9. Place three meatballs on each roll and spoon sauce over. Serve immediately.

Per Serving: 718 calories; fat 35g; 13g; protein 48g; carbs 54g;

CHICKEN POT PIE

Serve 8 / Prep time: 20 mins/ Cook time: 60 mins

- 1 pound skinless, boneless chicken breast halves - cubed
- 1 cup sliced carrots
- ½ cup sliced celery
- ⅓ cup chopped onion
- ½ teaspoon salt
- ¼ teaspoon celery seed
- ⅔ cup milk
- 1 cup frozen green peas
- ⅓ cup butter
- ⅓ cup all-purpose flour
- ¼ teaspoon black pepper
- 1 ¾ cups chicken broth
- 2 (9 inch) unbaked pie crusts

1. Preheat the oven to 425 degrees F (220 degrees C). Combine chicken, carrots, peas, and celery in a saucepan; add water to cover and bring to a boil. Boil for 15 minutes, then remove from the heat and drain.
2. While the chicken is cooking, melt butter in another saucepan over medium heat. Add onion and cook

until soft and translucent, 5 to 7 minutes.

3. Stir in flour, salt, pepper, and celery seed. Slowly stir in chicken broth and milk. milk and broth added to the seasoned roux
4. Reduce heat to medium-low and simmer until thick, 5 to 10 minutes. Remove from heat and set aside.
5. Place chicken and vegetables in the bottom pie crust. Pour hot liquid mixture over top.
6. Cover with top crust, seal the edges, and cut away any excess dough. Make several small slits in the top crust to allow steam to escape.
7. Bake in the preheated oven until the pastry is golden brown and the filling is bubbly 30 to 35 minutes. Cool for 10 minutes before serving. Serve immediately and enjoy!

Per Serving: Calorie: 412 / Carbs: 30g / Protein: 18g / Fat: 24g / Fiber: 3g

SLOPPY JOE

Serves: 6 / Prep time: 5 mins/ Cook time: 20 mins

- 1 pound lean ground beef
- ¼ cup chopped green bell pepper
- 1 tablespoon brown sugar, or to taste
- ½ teaspoon garlic powder
- 6 hamburger buns, split
- ¼ cup chopped onion
- ¾ cup ketchup, or to taste
- 1 teaspoon yellow mustard, or to taste
- salt and ground black pepper to taste

1. Heat a large skillet over medium heat. Cook and stir lean ground beef in the hot skillet until some of the fat starts to render, 3 to 4 minutes.
2. Add onion and bell pepper; continue to cook until vegetables have softened and beef is cooked through, 3 to 5 more minutes.
3. Stir in ketchup, brown sugar, mustard, and garlic powder; season with salt and pepper
4. Reduce heat to low and simmer for 20 to 30 minutes. Divide the meat mixture evenly among hamburger buns.

Per Serving: Calorie: 243 / Carbs: 11g / Protein: 14g / Fat: 16g

CLASSIC MEATLOAF

Serves 10 / Prep time: 30 mins/ Cook time: 1hr

- 1 medium carrot, coarsely chopped
- ½ medium onion, coarsely chopped
- 4 white mushrooms, coarsely chopped
- 2 ½ pounds ground chuck
- 1 large egg, beaten
- 2 teaspoons salt
- ½ teaspoon cayenne pepper
- 2 tablespoons brown sugar
- 2 tablespoons Dijon mustard
- 1 rib celery, coarsely chopped
- ½ medium red bell pepper, coarsely chopped
- 3 cloves garlic, coarsely chopped
- 1 tablespoon Worcestershire sauce
- 1 teaspoon dried Italian herbs
- 1 teaspoon ground black pepper
- 1 cup plain bread crumbs
- 2 tablespoons ketchup
- 1 teaspoon Sriracha sauce, or to taste

1. Preheat the oven to 325 degrees F (165 degrees C). Line a baking dish with lightly greased foil.
2. Place carrot, celery, onion, bell pepper, mushrooms, and garlic in a food processor; pulse until very finely chopped, almost to a purée.
3. Transfer to a large mixing bowl. Overhead shot of a food processor with puréed vegetables for meatloaf
4. Add ground chuck to the vegetables, along with Worcestershire sauce, egg, Italian herbs, salt, black pepper, and cayenne.
5. Mix gently with a wooden spoon until the ingredients are just combined. Sprinkle in bread crumbs and gently mix with your fingertips until just combined; don't overmix.
6. Shape the mixture into a loaf, about 4 inches high by 6 inches across. Place in the prepared baking pan. Bake in the preheated oven just until the meatloaf is hot, about 15 minutes.
7. Stir brown sugar, ketchup, Dijon, and Sriracha for glaze in a small bowl until brown sugar has dissolved.
8. Remove the meatloaf from the oven. Spoon glaze on the top of the meatloaf with the back of a spoon, then pull a tiny bit of glaze down the sides.
9. Return to the oven, and bake until no longer pink inside, 45 to 75 more minutes. Serve hot and enjoy!

Per Serving: Calories 284 / Fat 15g / Carbs 15g / Protein 22g / Fiber: 1g

SHRIMP SCAMPI PASTA

Serves 6 / Prep time: 20 mins/ Cook time: 20 mins

- 1 (16 ounces) package of linguine pasta
- 2 tablespoons extra-virgin olive oil
- 2 cloves garlic, minced
- 1 pound shrimp, peeled and deveined
- ½ cup dry white wine
- 2 tablespoons butter
- ¼ cup finely chopped fresh parsley leaves
- 2 tablespoons butter
- 2 shallots, finely diced
- 1 pinch red pepper flakes (Optional)
- 1 pinch kosher salt and freshly ground pepper
- 1 lemon, juiced
- 2 tablespoons extra-virgin olive oil
- 1 teaspoon extra-virgin olive oil, or to taste

1. Bring a large pot of salted water to a boil; cook linguine in boiling water until nearly tender, 6 to 8 minutes. Drain.
2. Dry spaghetti pasta in a large pot with boiling water
3. Melt 2 tablespoons butter with 2 tablespoons olive oil in a large skillet over medium heat.
4. Pan cooking small cubes of butter that are melting with 3 other minced ingredients in bowls on the side
5. Cook and stir shallots, garlic, and red pepper flakes in the hot butter and oil until shallots are translucent, 3 to 4 minutes.
6. Season shrimp with kosher salt and black pepper; add to the skillet and cook until pink, stirring occasionally, 2 to 3 minutes. Remove shrimp from the skillet and keep warm.
7. Pour white wine and lemon juice into the skillet and bring to a boil while scraping the browned bits of food off of the bottom of the skillet with a wooden spoon.
8. Melt 2 tablespoons butter in a skillet, stir 2 tablespoons olive oil into the butter mixture, and bring to a simmer.
9. Toss linguine, shrimp, and parsley in the butter mixture until coated; season with salt and black pepper. Drizzle with 1 teaspoon olive oil to serve. Serve hot and enjoy!

Per Serving: Calories 511 / 19gFat / 58gCarbs / 22g Protein / Fiber: 4g

BAKED CHICKEN DRUMSTICKS WITH BBQ SAUCE

Serves 3 / Prep time: 10 mins/ Cook time: 40 mins

- 1 ½ pounds chicken drumsticks
- 1 teaspoon salt
- ½ teaspoon paprika
- ¼ teaspoon onion powder
- 1 ½ cups barbeque sauce , or more to taste
- ¼ cup extra-virgin olive oil
- ½ teaspoon freshly ground black pepper
- ¼ teaspoon garlic powder
- ¼ teaspoon cayenne pepper

1. Preheat the oven to 400 degrees F (200 degrees C). Line a baking sheet with foil.
2. Mix olive oil, salt, pepper, paprika, garlic powder, onion powder, and cayenne in a large bowl. Add drumsticks and toss to coat. Spread out on the prepared baking sheet.
3. Bake in the preheated oven for 20 minutes. Remove from the oven and brush with barbeque sauce. Bake for 7 to 8 minutes.
4. Flip drumsticks, brush with barbeque sauce and bake for an additional 7 to 8 minutes.
5. Set an oven rack about 6 inches from the heat source and turn on the oven's broiler.
6. Brush drumsticks with more barbeque sauce and broil for 3 to 4 minutes.
7. Flip drumsticks, brush with barbeque sauce, and broil until chicken is no longer pink at the bone and the juices run clear for 3 to 4 more minutes.

Per Serving: 725Calories / 39gFat / 46g Carbs / 44g Protein / Fiber: 1g

VEGGIE-LOADED NACHOS

Serves 6 / Prep time: 15 mins/ Cook time: 10 mins

- 8 ounces sturdy tortilla chips
- 1 can (15 ounces) pinto beans, rinsed and drained, or 1 ½ cups cooked pinto beans
- 1 packed cup (4 ounces) shredded cheddar cheese

- 1 packed cup (4 ounces) of shredded Monterey Jack cheese or additional cheddar
- 1 medium red bell pepper, finely chopped
- ⅓ cup crumbled feta cheese
- Pickled jalapeños, to taste
- Avocado dip, thinned with water until it reaches a drizzly consistency or guacamole
- ⅓ cup chopped green onions
- 2 radishes, chopped
- 2 tablespoons chopped cilantro

1. Preheat the oven to 400 degrees Fahrenheit. Line a baking sheet with parchment paper.
2. Place handfuls of chips on the baking sheet and distribute evenly, minimizing the gaps between chips. Set aside.
3. Sprinkle the prepared pan of chips generously and evenly with the beans, followed by the shredded cheese, bell pepper, crumbled feta, and pickled jalapeños (use more if you love jalapeños, less if you don't).
4. Bake until the cheese is melted and bubbling, about 9 to 13 minutes. Remove the nachos from the oven and set aside.
5. While the nachos are baking, make the avocado sauce and prepare the garnishes.
6. Once the nachos are out of the oven, drizzle the avocado sauce on top as shown—any extra can be served on the side. Sprinkle the nachos with chopped green onion, radish and cilantro. Serve immediately, with salsa on the side.

Per Serving: Calories: 820 / Carbs: 65g / Protein: 8g / Fat: 44g / Fiver: 8g

SPINACH AND FETA STUFFED CHICKEN BREAST

Serves 4 / Prep time: 25 mins/ Cook time: 35 mins

- 1 tablespoon olive oil
- 1 cup chopped yellow onion
- 2 tablespoons chopped fresh dill
- 5 ounces baby spinach
- 2 ounces crumbled feta cheese (about 1 / 2 cup)
- 4 (6 ounces) skinless, boneless chicken breasts
- ½ teaspoon kosher salt
- ¼ teaspoon black pepper
- 1 ½ teaspoons olive oil

1. Heat a large skillet over medium heat. Add 1 tablespoon of olive oil to the pan. Add onion; cook for 8 minutes, stirring frequently.
2. Remove pan from heat; stir in dill, spinach, and feta cheese. Cool for 10 minutes. Cut a horizontal slit through the center of each chicken breast to form a pocket.
3. Stuff each pocket evenly with the spinach mixture. Close pockets with toothpicks. Sprinkle it with salt and pepper.
4. Heat skillet over medium-high heat. Add 1 1 / 2 teaspoons of olive oil to the pan. Add chicken; cook for 4 minutes.
5. Turn chicken. Cover the pan, reduce heat to medium, and cook for 5 minutes or until the chicken is done.

Per Serving: Calorie: 426 / Carbs: 4.7g / Protein: 33g / Fat: 8.4g / Fiber: 2.2g

Chapter VIII Appetizer Recipes

CAPRESE SKEWERS WITH BALSAMIC GLAZE

Serves 12 / Prep time: 15mins

- 36 red cherry tomatoes
- 36 small basil leaves
- 1 teaspoon Italian seasoning
- salt and pepper to taste
- 24 bite-sized fresh mozzarella balls
- 1 1 / 2 tablespoons olive oil
- 1 1 / 2 tablespoons balsamic glaze
- 12 6-inch skewers

1. In a small bowl, mix the olive oil, Italian seasoning, and salt and pepper to taste.
2. Add the mozzarella balls to the bowl and toss them to coat.
3. Thread the tomatoes, basil, and mozzarella balls onto the skewers alternating between them.
4. Place the balsamic glaze in a small plastic bag with one corner snipped off. Drizzle the balsamic over the skewers, and serve immediately

Per Serving: Calories: 170kcal / Carbs: 3g / Protein: 11g / Fat: 14g / Fiber: 1g

SPINACH AND ARTICHOKE DIP

Serves: 8 / Prep time: 10 mins / Cook time 20 mins

- 8 oz. cream cheese, well softened
- 1 / 4 cup mayonnaise
- 2 / 3 cup (76g) finely shredded parmesan cheese
- 1 / 2 cup (56g) finely shredded mozzarella cheese
- 1 (14 oz) can quartered artichoke hearts, can liquid drained, squeeze artichokes to drain excess liquid, chopped
- 6 oz. frozen spinach, thawed, squeezed to drain excess liquid
- 1 / 4 cup sour cream
- 1 garlic clove, minced (1 tsp)
- Pepper, to taste

1. Preheat oven to 350 degrees. Spray a small (1 quart) baking dish with non-stick cooking spray.
2. In a mixing bowl stir together cream cheese, sour cream, mayonnaise, garlic, parmesan, mozzarella, and pepper.
3. Stir in artichokes and spinach. Spread the mixture evenly into the prepared baking dish.
4. Bake in preheated oven until heated through and melts about 20 minutes.
5. Serve warm with tortilla chips, crackers, or toasted baguette slices

Per Serving: Calories 242 kcal / Carbs 6g / Protein 8g / Fat 20g / Fiber 2g

BRUSCHETTA WITH TOMATO AND BASIL

Serves: 26 / Prep time: 15 mins/ Cook time: 20 mins

- 6-7 ripe plum or beefsteak tomatoes, diced
- 1 / 4 small red onion, chopped
- 2 tbsp balsamic vinegar
- 6-8 fresh basil leaves, chopped
- Freshly ground black pepper to taste
- 1-2 garlic cloves, peeled
- 2 cloves garlic, minced
- 1 tbsp extra virgin olive oil
- Olive oil spray
- Kosher salt
- 16 oz baguette or French bread

1. Combine tomatoes, chopped garlic, red onion, vinegar, oil, salt, pepper, and basil. Set aside.
2. Slice bread into 1 / 2-inch thick slices. Place on a tray and spray lightly with olive oil.
3. Toast bread under broiler, until golden, watching closely not to let it burn.
4. When bread is toasted, rub each piece with whole garlic clove. Place bread on a platter and top with tomato mixture.
5. Serve immediately or the bread will become soggy.

Per Serving: Calories: 49.6 kcal / Carbs: 9.1 g / Protein: 1.1 g / Fat: 0.6 g / Sodium: 2 mg / Fiber: 0.5 g

MINI MEATBALLS WITH SWEET AND SPICY GLAZE

Serves 8 / Prep time: 5 mins/ Cook time: 25 mins

- 2 lbs lean ground turkey
- 2 eggs
- 1 / 2 teaspoon garlic powder
- 1 / 2 teaspoon black pepper

For the sauce:

- 1 / 4 cup Sriracha
- 3 tablespoons rice vinegar
- 1 Tbsp grated fresh ginger
- 1 / 2 teaspoon sesame oil

- 1 cup whole wheat panko breadcrumbs
- 1 / 4 cup green onions, chopped
- 1 / 2 teaspoon salt

- 3 tablespoons reduced-sodium soy sauce
- 3 tablespoons honey
- 3 cloves garlic, minced

1. Preheat the oven to 375 degrees F.
2. In a large bowl, mix turkey, breadcrumbs, eggs, green onions, garlic powder, and salt / pepper until well combined. Shape mixture into 1 1 / 2-inch balls and place spaced apart on prepared baking sheets lightly sprayed with cooking spray.
3. Bake meatballs for 20 to 25 minutes, or until browned and cooked through.
4. While the meatballs are baking, combine all the ingredients for the sauce in a small saucepan and bring to a boil over medium heat, whisking continuously.
5. Reduce heat and simmer for 8 to 10 minutes (the sauce will start to thicken) then toss with the meatballs.
6. Serve immediately over brown rice and top with green onions and a few sesame seeds. Enjoy!

Per Serving: Calorie: 296 kcal / Carbs: 18.7g / Protein: 26.9g / Fat: 10.8g / Fiber: 1.4g

STUFFED MUSHROOMS WITH CREAM CHEESE AND HERBS

Serves 6 / Prep time:15 mins/ Cook Time:25 mins

- 12 whole fresh mushrooms, tough ends trimmed
- 1 tablespoon minced garlic
- ¼ cup grated Parmesan cheese
- ¼ teaspoon onion powder

- 1 tablespoon vegetable oil
- 1 (8-ounce) package of cream cheese, softened
- ¼ teaspoon ground black pepper
- ¼ teaspoon cayenne pepper

1. Preheat the oven to 350 degrees F (175 degrees C). Prepare a baking sheet with cooking spray.
2. Clean mushrooms with a damp paper towel. Carefully break stems from mushrooms.
3. Finely chop stems and set caps aside.Heat oil in a large skillet over medium heat.
4. Fry chopped mushroom stems and garlic in hot oil until any moisture has disappeared, taking care not to burn the garlic, 3 to 5 minutes.
5. Spread mushroom mixture into a bowl to cool completely, about 10 minutes.
6. Stir cream cheese, Parmesan cheese, black pepper, onion powder, and cayenne pepper into the cooled mushroom mixture until very thick and completely mixed.
7. Use a small spoon to fill each mushroom cap with a generous amount of stuffing. Arrange stuffed mushrooms on the prepared cookie sheet.
8. Bake in the preheated oven until piping hot and liquid starts to form under each cap, about 20 minutes

Per Serving: Calories: 176 / Carbs: 3g / Protein:5g / Fat: 16g

SHRIMP COCKTAIL

Serves 4 / Prep time: 15 mins/ Cook time: 23 mins

- 10 cups cold water
- 2 stalks celery, quartered
- 1 head garlic, halved
- 1 / 2 bunch parsley
- 2 bay leaves
- 1 tablespoon kosher salt
- Lemon wedges
- 1 lemon, zest finely grated and juiced

- 2 medium carrots, quartered
- 1 large onion, quartered
- 1 lemon, halved
- 5 sprigs fresh thyme
- 1 pound medium or large shrimp, in the shell, rinsed
- The cocktail Sauce, recipe follows
- 1 cup ketchup
- 4 teaspoons prepared horseradish, or to taste, drained

- 1 / 4 teaspoon Worcestershire sauce
- Hot sauce, to taste

1. Put the water, carrot, celery, onion, garlic, lemon, parsley, thyme, and bay leaves in a pot and bring to a boil over high heat.
2. Lower the heat to a simmer, set a cover on top slightly ajar, and cook for 10 to 30 minutes.
3. Drop the shrimp into the liquid and turn off the heat. Cook the shrimp, stirring occasionally, until they curl and turn pink, about 2 to 2 ½ minutes for medium shrimp, and 3 minutes for large ones.
4. Drain and cool to room temperature. Peel the shrimp and remove the vein along the curve of the shrimp, if desired. Refrigerate if not serving right away. If refrigerated, bring the shrimp to room temperature 20 minutes before serving.
5. To serve, put the cocktail sauce in a medium bowl and surround it with the shrimp, or loop the shrimp over the edge of an individual cocktail glass and top with the sauce. Garnish with the lemon and serve.
6. To devein the shrimp before cooking, hold a shrimp between the thumb and forefinger with the rounded side of the shrimp upward.
7. Place the pointed end of a wooden skewer at the junction of the second and third segments of the shrimp shell, about 1 / 8 inch down from the top.
8. Gently push the skewer through the shell and then lift it to remove the vein.
9. Combine the ketchup, lemon zest and juice, horseradish, and Worcestershire sauce in a small bowl. Add hot sauce, if desired. Mix well, then refrigerate until ready to serve

Per servings: Calories / 152 kcal / Carbs: 23g / Protein: 17g / Fat: 1g / Fiber: 3g

BUFFALO CAULIFLOWER BITES

Serves: 4 / Prep time: 15 mins/ Cook Time: 30 mins

- 1 cup water
- ½ teaspoon garlic powder, or to taste
- 2 heads cauliflower, cut into bite-size pieces
- ½ cup hot pepper sauce
- ¾ cup gluten-free baking flour
- salt and ground black pepper to taste
- 2 tablespoons butter
- 1 teaspoon honey

1. Preheat the oven to 450 degrees. Lightly grease a baking sheet with cooking spray.
2. Whisk together water, flour, garlic powder, salt, and pepper in a large bowl until the batter is smooth and somewhat runny.
3. Water, flour, garlic powder, salt, and pepper whisked together in a large bowl until smooth and runny.
4. Add cauliflower pieces to batter and mix until evenly coated; spread onto the prepared baking sheet.
5. Cauliflower pieces were added to the mixture and then placed on a baking sheet. Bake in the preheated oven until lightly browned, 20 to 25 minutes. Set aside.
6. Melt butter in a saucepan over medium heat. Remove from heat; stir in hot pepper sauce and honey until smooth.
7. Butter, hot pepper sauce, and honey mixed until smooth.Brush the hot sauce mixture over each cauliflower piece, repeating until all is used.
8. Return to the oven and bake until cauliflower is browned about 10 minutes. Let cool for 10 to 15 minutes before serving.

Per Serving: 218 Calories / Carbs: 36g / Protein: 9g / Fat: 7g

GUACAMOLE WITH TORTILLA CHIPS

Serves 16 / Prep time: 10 mins/ Cook Time: 10 mins

- 8 (6-inch) corn tortillas
- ½ teaspoon salt
- 3 tomatillos
- ⅓ cup chopped plum tomato
- 1 tablespoon fresh lime juice
- 2 ripe peeled avocados, seeded and coarsely mashed
- 2 jalapeño peppers, seeded and finely chopped
- 1 garlic clove, minced
- Cooking spray
- ½ teaspoon chipotle chile powder (such as McCormick)
- ⅓ cup chopped onion
- 3 tablespoons chopped fresh cilantro
- ¾ teaspoon salt

1. Preheat the oven to 375 °. Cut each tortilla into 8 wedges; arrange tortilla wedges in a single layer on 2

baking sheets coated with cooking spray.
2. Sprinkle wedges with 1 / 2 teaspoon salt and chile powder; lightly coat wedges with cooking spray.
3. Bake at 375° for 12 minutes or until wedges are crisp and lightly browned. Cool for 10 minutes.
4. To prepare guacamole, peel papery husk from tomatillos; wash, core, and finely chop.
5. Combine tomatillos, onion, and remaining ingredients; stir well. Serve guacamole with chips.
Per Serving: 57 Calories / fat 2.6g / Protein 1.2g / Carbs 8.3g; / Fiber 1.7g

DEVILED EGGS WITH SMOKED PAPRIKA

Serves: 12 / Prep time: 15 mins/ Total Time: 40 mins

- 6 large eggs
- 2 Tbsp. mayonnaise
- 1 tsp. yellow mustard
- 1 / 4 tsp. black pepper
- Ice
- 1 1 / 2 Tbsp. sweet or dill pickle relish
- 1 / 4 tsp. kosher salt
- Paprika (optional)

1. Fill a large pot with water; bring to a boil over high. Carefully lower eggs into boiling water; cook, undisturbed, for 11 minutes, 30 seconds.
2. Meanwhile, fill a large bowl halfway with ice; add water to cover. Set the ice bath aside.
3. Using a slotted spoon, immediately transfer cooked eggs from boiling water to an ice bath. Let stand until completely cooled, at least 5 minutes.
4. Working with 1 egg at a time, firmly tap on a flat surface until cracks form all over the shell. Peel under cold running water. Cut eggs in half lengthwise; remove yolks. Set egg white halves aside.
5. Using a fork, mask together yolks and mayonnaise in a medium bowl. Add relish, mustard, salt, and pepper; stir well to combine.
6. Spoon or pipe about 1 tablespoon filling into each egg white half. Garnish with paprika, if desired. Serve immediately.
Per Serving: Calories 140 / Carbs:10g / Protein:12g / Fat 12g / Fiber: 2g

GREEK SPANAKOPITA TRIANGLES

Serves: 10 / Total time: 35 Min

- 1 Egg
- Vegetable Oil125 ml (3 / 5 cup)
- salt 1 tsp
- Spinach
- Phyllo dough
- poppy seeds, for garnishing
- Milk 125 ml (1 / 2 cup)
- Water 2 tbsp
- Feta cheese
- salt and pepper to taste
- 3 rolls
- egg yolk, for brushing

1. Make the egg-wash mixture first. Mix the egg, milk, oil, water, and salt in a bowl, and set aside. In another clean bowl, mix the feta cheese and cooked spinach.
2. Lay a sheet of filo pastry on a clean surface and brush a little bit of the egg wash over the phyllo sheets. Repeat the process twice until you have a total of three layers.
3. Pour the feta and spinach over the filo pastry. Roll from one end to the other to obtain a long strip.
4. Use a large knife to cut the phyllo pastries into triangles and place them on a baking tray. Brush each triangle with egg yolk. Sprinkle with poppy seeds and bake at 180ºC (356°F) for 15 minutes.
5. For extra crispiness, don't leave out the butter in between the layers. For extra creaminess, add 1 / 3 cup of ricotta to the filling.
6. To make the spanakopita triangles ahead of time, make the filling and assemble the triangles on a baking sheet.
7. Cover tightly with plastic wrap and refrigerate overnight. Bake adding 5 to 10 minutes to the cooking time.
Per Serving: Calorie: 45 / Carbs: 1g / Protein: 3g / Fat: 3g / Fiber: 1g

BACON-WRAPPED DATES WITH GOAT CHEESE

Serves: 8 / Prep time: 5 mins/ Cook Time: 15 mins

- 12 ounces Medjool dates, pitted
- 4 ounces soft goat cheese

- 16 ounces bacon slices, halved
1. Preheat oven to 350°F. Slice a small slot into the side of each date and stuff it with goat cheese.
2. Wrap each date with a half-slice of bacon and poke a toothpick through.
3. Place stuffed dates on a baking sheet and roast for about 8 minutes.
4. Flip dates over and cook for an additional 5 to 8 minutes. Serve warm.

MINI QUICHES WITH SPINACH AND FETA

Serves: 18 / Prep time: 20mins/ Cook TIME18mins

- 4 sheets of puff pastry thawed
- 1 cup tasty cheese 90 grams
- 100 grams of feta crumbled
- ½ cup of milk 130 grams
- ½ teaspoon salt
- 100 grams of baby spinach leaves
- ½ cup parmesan cheese 50 grams
- 8 eggs
- 1 tablespoon onion flakes
- ¼ teaspoon pepper

1. Preheat your oven to 200 degrees Celsius (fan-forced). Remove the pastry from the freezer and allow it to thaw slightly.
2. Grate the tasty and parmesan cheese and set aside until needed.
3. In a large jug, whisk together the milk eggs, and onion flakes and add a sprinkle of salt and pepper.
4. Lightly grease 2 x muffin tins, and using a 12cm round cookie cutter, cut circles of pastry and gently mold them into the muffin tins – you will make approximately 18 quiches.
5. Equally divide the baby spinach leaves, feta, tasty, and parmesan cheese between the pastry cases and gently pour over the egg and milk mixture.
6. Place the two oven trays into your pre-heated oven and bake for 18 minutes, or until the filling is golden.
7. Leave the mini quiches in the trays for 5 minutes to cool slightly and then transfer to a wire rack to cool completely

Per Serving: Calories: 385kcal / Carbs: 26g / Protein: 10g / Fat: 27g / Fiber: 1g

CRISPY BAKED CHICKEN WINGS WITH HONEY MUSTARD SAUCE

Serves 2 / Prep time: 10 mins/ Cook time: 45 mins

- 2 1 / 2 – 3 lbs. of chicken wings (drumettes and wings)
- 1 teaspoon of paprika
- 1 / 2 teaspoon of chipotle chili powder
- 1 tablespoon of canola oil
- Honey Mustard Sauce:
- 1 / 2 cup of honey
- 1 / 2 cup of Dijon mustard (I use stone ground mustard because I like the texture)
- 1 / 2 teaspoon of ground mustard
- 1 teaspoon of garlic powder
- 1 / 2 teaspoon of ground cinnamon
- optional garnish: green onions, sesame seeds

- 2 tablespoons of butter

1. Preheat oven to 400 degrees. Pat chicken wings dry and place in a large bowl.
2. In a small bowl mix paprika, garlic powder, chipotle chili powder, and ground cinnamon.
3. Sprinkle seasoning mixture over chicken wings and then add canola oil, and toss to coat all the wings.
4. Add a wire rack to a baking sheet and evenly spread chicken wings out on a wire rack. Bake wings for 20 minutes.
5. Remove the pan from the oven, flip the chicken wings, and bake for an additional 20-25 minutes.
6. In the meantime, heat a small pot to medium-high heat. Add in mustard, honey, ground mustard, and butter. Stir until butter is melted and the sauce is warm.
7. Add cooked chicken wings to a large bowl with the honey mustard sauce, and toss the chicken wings around with the sauce until all the wings are covered.
8. Garnish with sliced green onions and sesame seeds.

Per Servings: Calories: 278 kcal / Carbs: 12 g / Protein: 21g / Fat: 15 g

SMOKED SALMON ROLL-UPS

Servings: 12 / Prep time: 15 mins

- 2 tablespoons sesame seeds
- 8 ounces smoked salmon

- 1 / 2 cup cream cheese whipped
- 1 tablespoon lemon zest
- 1 / 2 cucumber matchstick
- 2 tablespoons chives minced + divided
- 1 / 2 avocado thinly sliced

1. Lay a piece of plastic wrap on the counter. Sprinkle plastic wrap with sesame seeds (2 tablespoons).
2. Place smoked salmon (8 ounces) over the sesame seeds, overlapping the slices to form a 10 x 6" rectangle.
3. Spread whipped cream cheese (1 / 2 cup) over the top of the smoked salmon. Sprinkle with (2 tablespoons) chives and (1 tablespoon) lemon zest.
4. Place sliced (1 / 2) avocado and (1 / 2) cucumbers along the long edge of the salmon, then use the plastic wrap to help roll the salmon over itself.
5. Toss roll up in the freezer for 10 minutes before slicing. Slice into 12 pieces, and enjoy!

Per Serving: Calories: 78kcal / Carbs: 2g / Protein: 5g / Fat: 6g / Fiber: 1g

TOMATO AND MOZZARELLA CROSTINI

Serves 16 / Prep time: 15 mins/ Cook time: 15 mins

- 1 loaf Italian bread or French bread I sliced 16 slices from it and had a little bit more remaining
- 20-24 Cherry Tomatoes sliced twice or thrice
- 1 ball Fresh mozzarella sliced thinly
- 5 cloves Garlic minced finely
- a handful Fresh basil leaves chopped
- ⅓ cup olive oil
- ¼ cup basil pesto

1. Preheat the oven to 350 F. Slice the cheese, tomatoes, and bread and keep them ready.
2. Finely mince the garlic cloves and add it to the olive oil.
3. Now brush both sides of the bread with the garlic / olive oil mixture and arrange them on a baking sheet.
4. Bake the bread slices until light golden brown and appear toasted. This will take about 4 to 5 minutes. Keep an eye on them as the bread could burn easily.
5. Now top the toasted bread slices with sliced cheese, cherry tomatoes, and basil pesto (or fresh basil, if using).
6. Bake for another 5 minutes or so until the cheese is melted and the bread is well-toasted.
7. Serve the Crostini with Cherry Tomatoes And Mozzarella warm!

Per Serving: Calories: 260kcal / Carbohydrates: 17g / Protein: 6g / Fat: 19g / Fiber: 1g

CRAB RANGOON

Serves: 18 / Prep time: 20 mins/ Cook time: 2 mins

- 5 ounces of canned crab meat drained (can be substituted with fresh or packaged crab)
- 4 ounces cream cheese softened
- 1 teaspoon Worcestershire sauce
- ½ teaspoon garlic powder
- Oil for frying
- 1 green onion finely sliced
- 1 teaspoon soy sauce optional
- 18 wonton wrappers

1. Preheat 1 inch of oil to 325°F over medium heat.
2. In a small bowl, gently combine crab meat, cream cheese, green onion, Worcestershire sauce, soy sauce (if using), and garlic powder.
3. Layout 3 wonton wrappers at a time. Place 2 teaspoons of the filling in the center of each.
4. Dab the edges with water and fold the two opposite corners together to form a triangle.
5. Wet the tips of the triangle and fold inward. Continue until all of your filling is used up.
6. Drop the wontons into the hot oil for 2-3 minutes or until brown and crispy. Drain on paper towels.

Per Serving: Calories: 71 / Carbohydrates: 4g / Protein: 2g / Fat: 4g

AVOCADO SALSA

Serves 8 / Prep time: 15 mins

- 6 medium Roma tomatoes (20 oz), seeded and diced
- 1 cup chopped red onion, chopped
- 1 large or 2 small jalapeños, seeded and chopped (1 / 4 cup. Leave seeds if you like heat)

- 3 medium avocados, semi-firm but ripe, peeled, cored and diced
- 3 Tbsp olive oil
- 1 clove garlic, finely minced
- 1 / 4 tsp freshly ground black pepper
- 3 Tbsp fresh lime juice
- 1 / 2 tsp salt (more or less to taste as desired)
- 1 / 2 cup loosely packed cilantro leaves, chopped

1. Place red onion in a strainer or sieve and rinse under cool water to remove harsh bite. Drain well.
2. Add to a mixing bowl along with diced tomatoes, jalapeños and avocados.
3. In a separate small mixing bowl whisk together olive oil, lime juice, garlic, salt, and pepper until the mixture is well blended.
4. Pour mixture over avocado mixture, add cilantro then gently toss mixture to evenly coat. Serve with tortilla chips or over Mexican entrees.

Per Serving: Calories 238 / Carbs 12g / Protein: 2g / Fat: 21g / Fiber: 7g

TERIYAKI CHICKEN SKEWERS

Serves 4 / Prep time: 1 hr/ Cook time: 30 mins

- 2 cloves garlic minced
- ½ tablespoon fresh ginger minced
- ½ teaspoon sesame oil
- Optional Topping:
- sesame seed
- 1 tablespoon rice vinegar
- 1 tablespoon honey
- 8 skewers
- chopped green onions

1. First, make the sauce: Combine cornstarch and water in a small bowl. In a medium saucepan, add the remaining ingredients along with the cornstarch / water mixture Stirring frequently, bring the sauce to a simmer.
2. Cook until the sauce lightly thickens. The sauce will be dark brown. Once the sauce has thickened up, remove it from the heat and let cool completely. (place in the fridge to speed up the process)
3. Once the sauce is completely cooled, place the cubed chicken in a large ziplock bag. Pour half of the sauce over the chicken and gently shake to coat the chicken. Let chicken marinate in the fridge for at least 30 minutes. Place remaining sauce aside for later.
4. When the chicken is done marinating, place your chicken on skewers and heat the grill to medium heat.
5. Once the grill is hot, place skewers on a lightly oiled grill. Turn the skewers every 3-4 minutes until the chicken is cooked through (internal temp 165 degrees), about 20-30 minutes.
6. During the last few turns baste with the remaining teriyaki sauce. Remove skewers from the grill and serve with chopped green onion and a sprinkle of sesame seeds(optional).

Per Serving: 2skewers / Calories: 390 kcal / Carbs: 28g / Protein: 46g / Fat: 10g

PIGS IN A BLANKET

Serves 8 / Prep time: 10 mins/ Cook time: 15 mins

- All-purpose flour, for surface
- 1 (12-oz.) package mini cocktail weiners
- Coarse salt
- 1 (8-oz.) tube crescent rolls
- 4 tbsp. melted unsalted butter

1. Preheat the oven to 375º. On a lightly floured surface, unrolled crescent sheets and tears were perforated. Cut each triangle into 3 smaller triangles.
2. Place 1 cocktail weiner on the thick side of each triangle, then gently roll to the thinner side.
3. Transfer to a medium baking sheet. Bush with butter and sprinkle with salt.
4. Bake pigs in a blanket until golden, 12 to 15 minutes.

Per Serving: Calories 275 / Carbs 14.2g / Protein 7.4g / Fat 3.5g / Fiber 0.2g

ARTICHOKE AND SPINACH STUFFED BREAD

Serves: 20 / Prep time: 20 mins/ Cook time: 20 mins

- 1 French Baguette
- 4 cloves Garlic, Minced
- 4 cups Baby Spinach Leaves
- 1 1 / 2 cups Shredded Mozzarella Cheese
- 1 / 2 tablespoon Olive Oil
- 14 ounces Artichoke Hearts, Drained and chopped
- 1 8-ounce package of Cream Cheese

1. Preheat the oven to 350°F. Cut the baguette into 3 even sections. Using a long knife, hollow out the inside of the baguette, removing the bread from the inside but being sure to leave some bread along the edges. Set aside.
2. In a large skillet set over medium heat, heat olive oil. Add garlic, artichoke hearts, and spinach.
3. Heat, stirring often until spinach has wilted. Add cream cheese and mozzarella cheese. Stir and allow the cheese to melt, stirring constantly. Once completely melted, remove from heat.
4. Using a small spoon, fill each piece of hollow baguette with the artichoke cheese mixture.
5. Line the filled bread pieces on a cutting board and gently cut into 1-inch pieces. Carefully keep the baguette together, transfer the sliced baguette to a large long piece of foil, and wrap.
6. Place the baguette onto a baking sheet and bake in a preheated oven for 20 minutes. Remove from the oven and serve warm.

Per Serving: Calories 149 / Carbs 15g / Protein 6g / Fat 4g / Fiber 1g

CUCUMBER CUPS WITH TZATZIKI AND CHERRY TOMATOES

Serves 8 / Prep time: 10 mins/ Cook time: 5 mins

- 2cucumbers
- 1cupchicken, cooked, chopped
- ⅓cupfeta cheese
- cilantro, chopped, to taste
- ½cupcherry tomatoes, chopped
- olives, to taste
- salt and pepper, to taste
- Greek dressing, to taste

1. In a bowl, mix the cherry tomatoes, chopped chicken, olives, feta cheese, greek dressing, salt and pepper.
2. Peel the cucumbers partially, leaving thick stripes of skin going down the entire length of the cucumber.
3. Trim the ends of the cucumbers and cut each cucumber into 1 to 1½-inch thick slices.
4. Scoop out the center of each slice with a melon baller or spoon, leaving a shell of flesh.
5. Scoop about 1 tablespoon of the chicken mixture into the cucumber cups.
6. Garnish with additional cilantro and feta, if desired. Serve and enjoy.

Per Serving: Calories: 68.46kcal / Carbs: 3.66g / Protein: 4.79 / Fat: 4.09g / Fiber: 0.62g

SWEET POTATO FRIES WITH GARLIC AIOLI

Serve 6 / Prep time: 10 mins/ Cook time: 20 mins

- 3 large sweet potatoes, peeled and cut into 1 / 4-1 / 2 inch strips
- 2 tbsp olive oil, extra virgin
- 1 tsp paprika
- 1 tsp kosher salt
- 1 cup mayonnaise
- 2 tbsp olive oil, extra virgin
- 1 tbsp fresh parsley
- 1 / 2 tsp black pepper
- 1 tbsp cornstarch
- 1 tsp garlic powder
- 1 / 2 tsp black pepper
- 2 tbsp lemon juice
- 1 1 / 2 tbsp garlic powder
- 1 tsp kosher salt
- 1 / 4 tsp cayenne pepper

1. Preheat the oven to 420°F. Line a baking sheet with parchment paper and set aside.
2. Add sweet potato strips to a large mixing bowl and sprinkle cornstarchtarch. cornstarch olive oil and stir potatoes until evenly coated.
3. Season potatoes with garlic, paprika, salt, and pepper, stirring to make sure each fry is well seasoned.
4. Add fries to the baking sheet, making sure there's space between each fry. Bake for 15 minutes.
5. Using a spatula, turn the fries over. Bake for an additional 15 minutes or until golden brown on top. Remove from the oven and serve while still warm with garlic aioli dipping sauce.
6. Add mayo, lemon juice, olive oil, garlic powder, fresh parsley, cayenne pepper, salt, and black pepper to the food processor. Blend until all ingredients are mixed well together. Refrigerate for 30 minutes (or more) and serve chilled.

Per Serving: calories: 499 kcal / Carbs: 38g Protein: 4g / Fat: 37g / Fiber: 6g

Chapter IX Sweet snacks and desserts Recipes

CHOCOLATE CHIP COOKIES

Serves 48 / Prep time: 20 mins/ Cook time: 10 mins

- 1 cup butter, softened
- 2 eggs
- 2 teaspoons hot water
- 2 cups semisweet chocolate chips
- 1 cup white sugar
- 2 teaspoons vanilla extract
- ½ teaspoon salt
- 1 cup packed brown sugar
- 1 teaspoon baking soda
- 3 cups all-purpose flour
- 1 cup chopped walnuts

1. Gather your ingredients, making sure your butter is softened, and your eggs are at room temperature.
2. a top-down view of all ingredients for the best chocolate chip cookies. Preheat the oven to 350 degrees F (175 degrees C).
3. Beat butter, white sugar, and brown sugar with an electric mixer in a large bowl until smooth. Mix butter, white sugar, and brown sugar in a mixing bowl
4. Beat in eggs, one at a time, then stir in vanilla. mix egg into cookie batter, one at a time. Dissolve baking soda in hot water. Add to batter along with salt.
5. Mix baking soda and water into the cookie batter. Stir in flour, chocolate chips, and walnuts.
6. flour, chocolate chips, and nuts mixed into the cookie batter. Drop spoonfuls of dough 2 inches apart onto ungreased baking sheets.
7. cookies dropped by the spoonful, two inches apart on a baking sheet. Bake in the preheated oven until the edges are nicely browned, about 10 minutes.
8. cookies baked until the edges are perfectly golden brown. Cool on the baking sheets briefly before removing to a wire rack to cool completely.
9. chocolate chip cookies cooling on a wire rack. Store in an airtight container or serve immediately and enjoy!

Per Serving: 146 Calories / 8g Fat / 19gCarbs / 2gProtein

FRUIT SALAD WITH HONEY-LIME DRESSING

Serve: 10 mins / Prep time: 20 mins

- 1 lb fresh strawberries, chopped
- 12 oz fresh blueberries
- 4 kiwis, peeled and chopped
- 2 bananas, sliced (optional)
- 1 / 4 cup honey
- 1 1 / 2 Tbsp fresh lime juice
- 1 lb chopped fresh pineapple,
- 12 oz red grapes, sliced into halves
- 3 mandarin oranges*
- Honey Lime Dressing
- 2 tsp lime zest (zest of 2 medium limes)

1. Add all fruit to a large mixing bowl. In a small mixing bowl, whisk together honey, lime zest, and lime juice.
2. Pour over fruit and toss to evenly coat, serve immediately.

Per Serving: Calorie: 163 kcal / Carbs: 41g / Protein: 1g / Fiber: 5g

RICE KRISPIE TREATS

Serves: 24 / Prep time: 10 mins/ Cook time: 5mins

- ¼ cup butter
- 4 cups miniature marshmallows
- 5 cups crispy rice cereal

1. Melt butter in a large saucepan over low heat. Overhead of melted butter in a pan with a measuring cup full of marshmallows off to the side.
2. Add marshmallows and stir until melted and well combined. Cook 2 minutes longer, stirring constantly. Remove from heat.
3. Stir in crispy rice cereal until well coated. Overhead of crispy rice cereal and melted marshmallows mixed in a pot.

4. Press the mixture evenly and firmly into a buttered 9x13-inch pan using a buttered spatula or waxed paper.
5. Overhead of crispy rice treats pressed into a baking pan. Cut into 2-inch squares when cool.

Per Serving: Calorie: 65 kcal / Carbs: 12g / Protein: 5g / Fat: 2g

CHOCOLATE COVERED STRAWBERRIES

Serves: 24 / Prep time: 15 mins/ Cook time: 5 mins

- 16 ounces milk chocolate chips
- 2 tablespoons shortening
- toothpicks
- 1 pound fresh strawberries with leaves

1. Melt the chocolate and shortening together. Dip the strawberries in the chocolate.
2. Allow the chocolate to harden. Insert toothpicks into the tops (stem ends) of strawberries.
3. Hold a strawberry with the toothpick and dip it into the chocolate mixture.
4. Turn the strawberry upside down and insert the toothpick into a Styrofoam block or place the strawberry on a sheet of waxed paper; allow the chocolate coating to cool. Repeat with remaining strawberries.

Per Serving: Calorie: 115 kcal / Carbs: 13g / Protein: 7g / Fat: 1g

APPLE SLICES WITH PEANUT BUTTER

Serve: 1 / Prep time: 3mins

- 1 apple thinly sliced
- 20 g peanut butter, 100%
- ¼ tsp cinnamon

1. Spread the apple slices on a plate. Drizzle the peanut butter over the apple slices. Sprinkle with cinnamon.

Per Serving: 283 calories / 32g carbs 8g of protein / 16g fat / 7 fiber

NO-BAKE ENERGY BITES

Serves: 24 / Prep time: 15 mins/ Cook time: 1hr

- 1 cup rolled oats
- ½ cup miniature semisweet chocolate chips
- ½ cup ground flax seed
- ½ cup crunchy peanut butter
- ⅓ cup honey
- 1 teaspoon vanilla extract

1. Stir oats, chocolate chips, flax seed, peanut butter, honey, and vanilla extract together in a bowl.
2. Roll dough into 24 balls with your hands. Arrange balls on a baking sheet and freeze until set about 1 hour.

Per Serving: 94 calories / 11g carbs / 3g protein / 5g fat / 2g fiber

CINNAMON SUGAR DONUTS

Serves: 50 / Prep time: 45 mins/ Cook time: 5 mins

- 230g whole milk, lukewarm
- 2 Tbsp granulated sugar
- 2 tsp active, dry yeast
- 425g all-purpose flour
- ½ tsp salt
- 1 large egg, at room temperature, lightly beaten
- 50g Filippo Berio Extra Light Olive Oil
- To fry - Filippo Berio Extra Light Olive Oil
- Cinnamon Sugar
- 100g granulated sugar
- 1 tbsp cinnamon (do less if you want these less spicy)
- ½ tsp ground cardamom (optional)
- Pinch of salt

1. In the bowl of a stand mixer fitted with the dough hook, combine the lukewarm milk, sugar, and yeast, and leave to stand for 5-10 minutes or until foamy.
2. Add the flour, salt, egg, and oil, and mix on low speed until the dough comes together. Continue to mix for a further 10-12 minutes until the dough is soft and smooth, and when a little is stretched, you can see light through it
3. Shape the dough into a ball and place it into a bowl. Cover the bowl with plastic wrap and place in the fridge for a minimum of 3 hours and up to overnight.
4. Turn the dough out onto a very lightly floured surface. Roll out to about ½" (1.2cm) thickness. Roll the dough out to about ½" (1.2cm) thick. Using a circle cutter (I used a 3 ¼" circle), cut out circles of dough. Cut holes from the middle of the circles using a 1" circle cutter.

5. Place each onto a square of parchment paper then place onto a baking sheet, leaving room between. Place the doughnut holes on the sheet to proof alongside the doughnuts.
6. Press together scraps, re-roll, and cut out more doughnuts, or cut up into pieces and proof alongside the doughnuts to fry as snacks (my preferred method).
7. Cover and leave the doughnuts to proof for a further 35 to 45 minutes. When you poke them lightly with your finger, it should leave a small indentation that springs back.
8. While the doughnuts are proofing, heat Filippo Berio Extra Light Olive Oil in a large heavy-bottomed pot (cast iron works great) or deep fryer. Heat the oil to 350°f / 180°c.
9. Place a wire rack over a baking sheet lined with parchment paper. Combine the ingredients for the cinnamon sugar and place into a shallow bowl.
10. Once the oil has come to temperature, test it with a few scraps of dough, or the wonkiest doughnut (see tips for frying in the body of the post). Gently lower the doughnuts, two at a time, into the hot oil. Leave on the parchment paper if you like - it will release when added to the oil and you can fish out with tongs.
11. Cook for about 3 minutes, flipping halfway through, until golden brown. Remove from the oil using a slotted spoon and place on a cooling rack.
12. Allow to cool for 30 seconds before tossing in the sugar. Repeat the process with the rest of the doughnuts. Allow to cool on a rack.

Per Serving: Calorie: 271 kcal / Carb: 33.7 / Protein: 4.1g / Fat: 18.9g / Fiber: 1g

MIXED BERRY PARFAIT

Serves 1 / Prep time: 5mins/ Cook time: 5 mins

- 1 / 3 cup low-fat plain yogurt
- 1 tablespoon maple syrup
- 2 tablespoons maple syrup
- 1 / 2 cup old-fashioned oats
- 1 / 4 cup raw sunflower seeds
- Nonstick cooking spray
- 1 / 3 cup fresh or frozen mixed berries
- 1 tablespoon Easy Homemade Granola, recipe below
- 1 teaspoon extra-virgin raw coconut oil
- 1 / 4 cup sliced raw almonds
- Kosher salt

1. Fill a small single-serving (6-ounce) container with a third of the yogurt. Top with a third of the berries. Drizzle 1 teaspoon of maple syrup over the berries.
2. Repeat two more times with the rest of the yogurt, berries, and maple syrup.
3. Pack the granola separately so that it can be mixed into the parfait when ready to eat. Pack the parfait with an ice pack or frozen juice box so that it stays cold until lunchtime.
4. Easy Homemade Granola. Heat an oven to 350 degrees F.
5. Heat the maple syrup with the coconut oil in a small skillet over medium-low heat, just to melt the oil.
6. While still warm, toss the maple syrup mixture together with the oats, almonds, sunflower seeds, and a pinch of salt in a medium bowl. Spray a baking sheet with the nonstick cooking spray.
7. Spread the granola on the sheet tray in a thin layer. Bake for a total of 20 minutes, tossing the granola halfway through. Let cool to room temperature and store in an air-tight container in the refrigerator for up to 1 month.

Per Serving: Calorie: 200 kcal / Carbs: 36g / Protein: 6g / Fat: 4.5g / Fiber: 2g

ALMOND JOY ENERGY BALLS

Serves 2 / Prep time: 10 mins

- 3 / 4 cup unsweetened coconut flakes (reserve 1 / 2 cup for rolling)
- 2 cups dates*
- 1 / 4 cup unsweetened cocoa powder
- 1 / 2 tsp vanilla extract (you can also use almond extract if you prefer)
- 1–2 tbsp unsweetened almond milk
- 2 cups raw almonds
- 1 / 4 tsp sea salt

1. Put 1 / 2 cup of coconut flakes into the food processor and process to break up the flakes slightly. Do not over-process or it will become coconut butter.
2. Remove flakes and set aside in a bowl.
3. Place dates in the food processor and process until they have broken up and then come together into a

ball.

4. Break up the date ball with your hands and add in almonds, cocoa powder, 1 / 4 cup of coconut flakes, and sea salt.
5. Process for several minutes, scraping down the sides as needed. Add in vanilla extract and 1 tbsp of almond milk.
6. Process until the mixture comes back together into a ball. If it doesn't do this, add in 1 more tablespoon of almond milk. It should look like the photo above.
7. Remove mixture from the food processor and roll into roughly 2 dozen balls. Roll each ball in the coconut flakes you processed earlier.
8. Optional: place balls on a baking sheet and flash freeze in the freezer for 15-20 minutes. This ensures the balls won't stick together when you place them in your container.
9. Store in an airtight container in the fridge for several weeks or the freezer for several months

Per Serving: Calorie: 160kcal / Carbs: 23g / Protein:3g / Fat / 8g

LEMON BARS

Serves 6 / Prep time: 10 minutes/ Cook Time: 40 minutes.

- Shortbread Crust
- 1 / 2 cup (100g) granulated sugar
- 1 / 2 teaspoon salt
- 2 cups + 2 Tablespoons (265g) all-purpose flour (spooned & leveled)
- Lemon Filling
- 6 Tablespoons (46g) all-purpose flour
- 1 cup (240ml) lemon juice (about 4 lemons)
- optional: confectioners' sugar for dusting.
- 1 cup (230g; 2 sticks) unsalted butter, melted
- 2 teaspoons pure vanilla extract
- 2 cups (400g) granulated sugar
- 6 large eggs

1. Preheat the oven to 325°F (163°C). Line the bottom and sides of a 9×13 glass baking pan (do not use metal) with parchment paper, leaving an overhang on the sides to lift the finished bars out. Set aside.
2. Make the mix the melted butter, sugar, vanilla extract, and salt together in a medium bowl. Add the flour and stir to completely combine. The dough will be thick.
3. Press firmly into the prepared pan, making sure the layer of crust is nice and even. Bake for 20-22 minutes or until the edges are lightly browned.
4. Remove from the oven. Using a fork, poke holes all over the top of the warm crust (not through the crust). A new step I swear by, this helps the filling stick and holds the crust in place. Set aside.
5. Sift the sugar and flour together in a large bowl. Whisk in the eggs, then the lemon juice until completely combined.
6. Pour filling over warm crust. Bake the bars for 22-26 mins. Remove bars from the oven and cool completely at room temperature.
7. Once cool, lift the parchment paper out of the pan using the overhang on the sides. Dust with confectioners' sugar and cut into squares before serving.

Per Serving: Calorie: 180 kcal / Carbs: 19g / Protein: 1.7g / Fat:6.1g / Fiber:0.3g

BANANA BREAD

Serves 1 / Prep time: 10 mins/ Cook Time: 65 mins.

- 2 cups (250g) all-purpose flour (spooned & leveled)
- 1 / 4 teaspoon salt
- 1 / 2 cup (8 Tbsp; 113g) unsalted butter, softened to room temperature
- 3 / 4 cup (150g) packed light or dark brown sugar
- 2 large eggs, at room temperature
- 1 / 3 cup (80g) plain yogurt or sour cream, at room temperature
- 2 cups (460g) mashed bananas (about 4 large ripe bananas)
- 1 teaspoon pure vanilla extract
- optional: 3 / 4 cup (100g) chopped pecans or walnuts.
- 1 teaspoon baking soda
- 1 / 2 teaspoon ground cinnamon

1. Adjust the oven rack to the lower third position and preheat the oven to 350°F (177°C). Lowering the oven rack prevents the top of your bread from browning too much, too soon.

2. Grease a metal 9×5-inch loaf pan with nonstick spray. Set aside. Whisk the flour, baking soda, salt, and cinnamon together in a medium bowl. Set aside.
3. Using a handheld or stand mixer fitted with a paddle or whisk attachment, beat the butter and brown sugar together on high speed until smooth and creamy, about 2 minutes.
4. With the mixer running on medium speed, add the eggs one at a time, beating well after each addition. Then beat in the yogurt, mashed bananas, and vanilla extract until combined.
5. With the mixer running on low speed, slowly beat the dry ingredients into the wet ingredients until no flour pockets remain. Do not over-mix. Fold in the nuts, if using.
6. Pour and spread the batter into the prepared baking pan. Bake for 60–65 minutes, making sure to loosely cover the bread with aluminum foil halfway through to prevent the top from getting too brown. checking every 5 minutes.
7. Remove the bread from the oven and allow the bread to cool in the pan set on a wire rack for 1 hour. Remove bread from the pan and cool bread directly on the wire rack until ready to slice and serve.
8. Cover and store banana bread at room temperature for 2 days or in the refrigerator for up to 1 week. Banana bread tastes best on day 2 after the flavors have settled together.

Per Serving: Calorie: 326 kcal / Carbs 55 g / Protein 4.3 g / Fat 11 g / Fiber 1.1 g

DARK CHOCOLATE-DIPPED PRETZELS

Serves 2 / Prep time: 20 mins

- 2 bags dark chocolate chips
- Chopped nuts for garnish
- Sprinkles for garnish
- Crushed cookies for garnish
- 1 bag of pretzels any variety
- Colored nonpareils for garnish
- Coconut for garnish

1. Melt chocolate in a double boiler over medium heat on the stovetop. Using tongs, or your fingers, quickly dip pretzels in chocolate allowing the excess to run off.
2. Place dipped pretzels on waxed paper-lined cookie sheets. Sprinkle with chopped nuts, colored sugars, or other toppings.
3. Allow to harden. You can refrigerate them for 20 minutes to speed this process up.
4. Once hardened, remove from sheets and store in a cool location, with waxed paper between layers.

Per Serving: Calories: 368 kcal / Carbohydrates: 38g / Protein: 6g / Fat: 21g / / Fiber: 3g

PUMPKIN SPICE MUFFINS

Serves 12 / Prep time: 15 minutes/ Cook Time: 21 minutes

- 1 and 3 / 4 cups (219g) all-purpose flour (spooned & leveled)
- 1 teaspoon baking soda
- 1 and 1 / 2 teaspoons pumpkin pie spice*
- 1 / 2 teaspoon salt
- 1 / 2 cup (100g) granulated sugar
- 1 and 1 / 2 cups (340g) canned pumpkin puree (not pumpkin pie filling)
- 2 large eggs
- 1 and 1 / 2 teaspoons ground cinnamon
- 1 / 4 teaspoon ground ginger
- 1 / 2 cup (120ml) vegetable oil (or melted coconut oil)
- 1 / 3 cup (67g) packed light or dark brown sugar
- 1 / 4 cup (60ml) milk (dairy or non-dairy)

1. Preheat oven to 425°F (218°C). Spray a 12-count muffin pan with nonstick spray or line it with cupcake liners.
2. In a large bowl, whisk the flour, baking soda, cinnamon, pumpkin pie spice, ginger, and salt together until combined. Set aside.
3. In a medium bowl, whisk the oil, granulated sugar, brown sugar, pumpkin puree, eggs, and milk together until combined.
4. Pour the wet ingredients into the dry ingredients, and then fold everything together gently just until combined and no flour pockets remain.
5. Spoon the batter into liners, filling them to the top.
6. Bake for 5 minutes at 425°F, then, keeping the muffins in the oven, reduce the oven temperature to 350°F (177°C).
7. Bake for an additional 16–17 minutes or until a toothpick inserted in the center comes out clean. The total time these muffins take in the oven is about 21–22 minutes, give or take.

8. Allow the muffins to cool for 5 minutes in the muffin pan before enjoying. Cover tightly and store at room temperature for up to 1 week.

Per Serving: Calorie: 219 kcal / Carbs 4.3g / Protein 0.5g / Fat 1.3g / Fiber 0.1g

OATMEAL RAISIN ENERGY BALLS

Servings: 12 / Prep time: 15 mins

- 1 cup old-fashioned rolled oats
- 2 tablespoons chia seeds
- A pinch of sea salt
- 1 / 4 cup honey
- 1 / 4 cup raisins
- 1 / 4 cup ground flaxseed
- 1 / 2 teaspoon ground cinnamon
- 1 / 2 cup creamy almond butter I use Justin's Vanilla Almond Butter
- 1 / 2 teaspoon vanilla extract

1. In a large bowl, combine the oats, ground flaxseed, chia seeds, cinnamon, and salt.
2. Place the almond butter in a small microwave-safe bowl. Heat in the microwave for 20-30 seconds. Stir until smooth.
3. Add the honey and vanilla extract to the melted almond butter. Stir until smooth.
4. Pour over the oat mixture and stir until well combined. Stir in the raisins.
5. Roll the mixture into small balls, about 1-2 tablespoons per ball. Place in an airtight container and keep refrigerated for up to 2 weeks.

Per Serving: 12g, Calorie / 148kcal, Carbs: 16g / Protein: 4g / Fat: 8g / Fiber: 3g

BERRY SORBET

Serves 4 / Prep time:15mins/ Cook Time 4hours

- 400 gm frozen mixed berries
- 2 tbsp honey
- 1 / 4 cup sugar
- 1 tsp vanilla extract

1. Combine all the ingredients in a strong blender or food processor. Blend till smooth. Add water, if it gets too tight but in very small quantities.
2. Pour into a container and freeze for a couple of hours.
3. Take out and beat the mixture using a hand beater to crush all icicles. Freeze for another two hours.
4. To scoop, keep out for 10 minutes. Scoop, serve, and enjoy!

Per Serving: Calorie: 84 kcal / Carbs: 21g / Protein: 0g / Fat: 1g /

PECAN PIE BARS

Serves: 36 / Prep time: 29 mins/ Cook time:45 mins

- 3 cups all-purpose flour
- ½ teaspoon salt
- 1 ½ cups light corn syrup
- 4 large eggs
- 1 ½ teaspoons vanilla extract
- ½ cup white sugar
- 1 cup butter or margarine
- 1 ½ cups white sugar
- 3 tablespoons butter or margarine, melted
- 2 ½ cups chopped pecans

1. In a large saucepan, combine the brown sugar, honey, butter, cream, and salt. Bring to a boil then reduce heat and simmer for 2 minutes.
2. Remove from heat and stir in vanilla and pecans, mixing until incorporated.
3. Pour hot pecan filling over your warm crust. Return to the oven and bake for another 20-25 minutes until the top is bubbling and turns caramel color.
4. Set the baking pan on a wire rack and cool completely to room temperature before cutting.
5. Once the pecan squares are at room temperature, loosen the edges if needed and use the parchment paper or foil to lift the bars out of the pan.
6. Transfer to a cutting board and cut into 2-inch squares. Serve at room temperature.

Per Serving: 261kcal calories / / 22g carbs / 2g protein / 19g fat

CHOCOLATE AVOCADO MOUSSE

Servings: 4 / Prep time: 5mins

- flesh of 2 ripe avocados (240g)
- 1 / 4 cup regular cocoa powder

- 1 / 4 cup Dutch cocoa OR melted chocolate chips
- 3-4 tbsp milk of choice
- 1 / 2 tsp pure vanilla extract
- 1 / 8 tsp salt
- sweetener of choice to taste
1. The version with the chocolate chips will be richer; the version with the Dutch cocoa (important to use Dutch) will be lower in fat and sugar.
2. Combine all ingredients in a blender or food processor until completely smooth.
3. If you're not using a liquid sweetener then you might want to add a little extra for a smoother consistency.

Per Serving: Calorie: 492 kcal / Carbs: 24.1g / Protein:8.8g / Fat: 52.4g

BLUEBERRY OATMEAL BARS

Serves: 15 / Prep time: 10 mins/ Cook time: 35 mins

- 1 cup old-fashioned rolled oats gluten-free if needed
- 3 / 4 cup white whole wheat flour or substitute all-purpose flour or, to make gluten-free, 1:1 baking flour
- 1 / 3 cup light brown sugar
- 1 / 2 teaspoon ground cinnamon
- 1 / 4 teaspoon kosher salt
- 6 tablespoons unsalted butter melted (or substitute melted coconut oil to make vegan / dairy-free)
- 2 cups fresh blueberries* about 10 ounces
- 1 teaspoon cornstarch
- 1 tablespoon freshly squeezed lemon juice from about 1 / 2 small lemon
- 1 tablespoon granulated sugar divided
- 1 / 2 cup powdered sugar sifted
- 1 / 2 teaspoon pure vanilla extract
- 1 tablespoon milk of any kind
1. Place a rack in the center of your oven and heat to 375 degrees F. Line an 8x8-inch baking pan with parchment paper so that the paper overhangs two sides like handles.
2. In a medium bowl, combine the oats, white whole wheat flour, brown sugar, cinnamon, and salt.
3. Pour in the melted butter and stir until it forms clumps and the dry ingredients are evenly moistened. Set aside 1 / 2 cup of the crumble mixture, then press the rest into an even layer in the bottom of the prepared pan.
4. Scatter half of the blueberries over the crust. Sprinkle the cornstarch evenly over the top, then sprinkle on the lemon juice and 1 / 2 tablespoon granulated sugar.
5. Scatter on the remaining berries, then the remaining 1 / 2 tablespoon sugar. Sprinkle the reserved crumbs evenly over the top. You will have some fruit showing through.
6. Bake the bars for 30 to 40 minutes, until the fruit is bubbly and the crumb topping smells toasty and looks golden. Place the pan on a wire rack to cool completely (you can speed this process along in the refrigerator).
7. While the bars cool, prepare the glaze: in a medium bowl, briskly whisk together the powdered sugar, vanilla, and milk until smooth.
8. Using the parchment paper handles, lift the bars from the pan. Drizzle with the glaze, slice, and serve.

Per Serving: CALORIES: 105kcal / CARBS: 15g / PROTEIN: 2g / FAT: 5g / FIBER: 2g

S'MORES DIP

Prep time: 5 MINS/ Cook TIME: 6 MINS

- 3 oz milk chocolate bars
- 25 large marshmallows
- 10 graham crackers
1. Preheat the oven to 450° F oven and grease your baking dish.
2. Add a layer of milk chocolate to your baking dish. Place a layer of marshmallows.
3. Bake in the preheated oven for 4 - 5 minutes or until the marshmallows are toasted. Cool: Let cool for 10 minutes.

Per Serving: Calories: 137 kcal / Carbohydrates: 24g / Protein: 2g / Fat: 4g / Fiber 1g

Made in the USA
Las Vegas, NV
04 February 2024

85226902R00046